THE Ultimate Interview

THE Ultimate

Interview

HOW TO GET IT,

GET READY, AND

GET THE JOB

YOU WANT

JOHN CAPLE, Ph.D.

DOUBLEDAY
New York Toronto London Sydney Auckland

PUBLISHED BY DOUBLEDAY
a division of Bantam Doubleday Dell Publishing Group, Inc.
666 Fifth Avenue, New York, New York 10103

DOUBLEDAY and the portrayal of an anchor
with a dolphin are trademarks of Doubleday,
a division of Bantam Doubleday Dell
Publishing Group, Inc.

Library of Congress Cataloging-in-Publication Data

Caple, John.
    The ultimate interview : how to get it, get ready, and
get the job you want / John Caple.—1st ed.
        p.   cm.
    1. Employment interviewing.   I. Title.
    HF5549.5.I6C36   1991
    650.14—dc20   90-38922
                                                           CIP

ISBN 0-385-26583-2

BOOK DESIGN BY BONNI LEON

ILLUSTRATION BY JACKIE AHER

FOR

KATHY AND TOM

MY CHILDREN, MY TEACHERS

Acknowledgments

This book began as a title. It was my wife's idea, as we talked by San Francisco Bay on a June afternoon in 1986. She soon forgot it, but it stayed with me, tenacious and challenging, this vision of the ultimate interview.

Along the way, I was blessed with help from writers, job seekers, and professionals. I am particularly grateful to Dick Bolles, Nathan Bricklin, Otto Butz, Tom Caple, George Conlan, Tom Day, Paul Hartzell, JoAnn Haymaker, Patti Hoffman, Tom Jackson, Nicki Johnson, Jim Kennedy, Jay Levinson, John Nicholas, Blair Ogden, Terry Pearce, Bill Rodgers, Mort Scott, Max Shapiro, Nan Talese, and Ellen Wallach.

Also to John Hart and my colleagues in his writing class. To Michael Larsen and Elizabeth Pomada, my literary agents. To Jerry Gross, who contributed ideas as well as sound editing. And to John Duff, who brought it all together at Doubleday.

To end at the beginning, I thank my wife, Anne, for thoughtful editing, practical wisdom, and moral support in creating a book to go with the title she conceived that afternoon by the bay.

Contents

PART ONE: **Focusing**

PART TWO: **Getting Ready**

PART THREE: **Getting Results**

A Promise to the Reader

If you read this book, you will learn:

- Nine steps to knowing what work is right for you
- Five bits of wisdom to get you started
- Five kinds of interviews that lead to a job
- Fifteen ways to get a job interview
- Five ways a résumé is effective and two ways it is not
- Eleven rules on how to dress for an interview
- Nine rules on how *not* to dress for an interview
- Three secrets for readying your mind
- Nine key gestures that reveal inner emotions
- Nine types of interviewers and how to respond to them
- Four kinds of final interviews and which to seek
- The most effective interview and how it works
- Four stages in an interview and how to handle each
- Four stages in interview problem-solving
- Five approaches to answering tough questions
- Seven difficult interview situations and how to respond
- Five powerful ways to close an interview
- Three follow-up strategies for after the interview
- Seven cardinal rules of interviewing

A Second Promise

If you apply the strategies in this book, you will find work that is right for you.

Who Wrote This Book and Why?

Interviewer: Tell us about yourself.

John Caple: You mean even the stuff my mother doesn't know?

Int: Tell us what's behind this book.

JC: Work is my passion; that's at the heart of it. Passion fueled by my own struggles and by the success I've had in pointing others to work that is right for them. I've hired people, fired people, and been fired myself. I've taken the wrong jobs, I've hired the wrong people. Just about any mistake, I've made it. And learned from it in ways that others find useful.

Int: Useful in what ways?

JC: Practical ways reflecting principles of human motivation, manageable ways that lead to action. Since the late seventies, I've been counseling people and leading career-change workshops. I've written about work—this is my third book—and talked to radio, TV, and live audiences about it. I've coached college students on getting jobs and company presidents on filling jobs. I've helped lots of people explore what is work—and what is play—and what is right for them.

Int: So who is this book for?

JC: For people looking for their first or second or even fourth or fifth job. For people who figure there must be a better way and want to know what it is. This book offers advice, examples, coaching. It offers both information and inspiration.

Int: And where does all this lead?

JC: To more people doing work that is right for them, with all kinds of rewards for themselves, those they serve, and others in their lives. My view is that we all benefit whenever one of us finds meaningful work. Each job is a stepping-stone on a path whose end we cannot see. My vision, and yours, of where our paths lead inspires the journey and adds significance to each footfall. Any other questions?

Int: Just one. When can you start?

Introduction

IMAGINE a crisp, clear morning not long after sunrise, as two people in different parts of the city prepare for the day ahead. Each lingers an extra moment in the shower, luxuriating in the steam and hot water, thinking, "This is my big day. This is the day I'll get offered that marketing job at the best company in town, working with great people, for more money than I ever dreamed about."

Two candidates out for one job, the same job—the dream job of their careers. Their hopes are high as they put on their newly laundered, freshly pressed, color-coordinated interview outfits. Each of these two people has the knowledge, skills, and enthusiasm to do the job. Each has allowed ample time to arrive a few minutes early for the appointment that may, just may, lead to the coveted job offer.

One of those two people will get the job.

One won't.

What will make the difference?

The successful candidate has thought long and hard about what work is right for him or her, asking tough questions, evaluating experiences and skills, values and passions. This person knows all that can be known, based on exhaustive internal exploration, about what tasks and missions are right for the unique gifts he or she brings to the world of work.

> *Efficiency is doing the work right. Effectiveness is doing the right work.*
>
> **Peter Drucker (paraphrased)**

The successful candidate knows all about interviewing: about impeccable preparation, how to begin an interview, and what to focus on during the interview. The successful candidate knows how to respond to different interviewer styles and to different lines of questioning. The successful candidate knows how to bring the interview to a satisfactory conclusion and what to do afterward.

The one who walks out with the job offer knows everything important about the industry, the company, the position being filled; about the people who work for the company and in the department, and even some who work for customers and competitors.

The winning candidate is getting the offer today as a result of knowing at least a dozen ways to get an interview. This is not an easy company to get into, and several approaches were required to arrive at this point.

The one who will walk out with the job knows how to read nonverbal messages from posture, gestures, and eye contact; how to interpret different speaking patterns and how to respond; when it is best to talk more slowly, or more forcefully, or more rapidly.

The successful candidate knows what interviewers want and how to give it to them, how to focus the conversation on what interviewers need when they are not sure what they want, and how to be as effective with interviewers who are inexperienced as with those who are highly skilled.

The candidate who walks out today thinking "I knew it would happen!" is the one who learned everything there was to know about interviewing.

The other candidate knows a lot too, but the knowledge was scattered or unclear or forgotten, not quite totally focused, which makes for less confidence and less poise. In the end, that made the difference between winning and losing.

This book is for those who want to be like the first candidate. It is for those who want the right job, the right career, and the right work in their lives. Picture that goal as three concentric circles, with the bull's-eye in the center:

The right job may be a part-time, temporary, or contractual assignment or it may be a forty-hour-a-week commitment leading to a long-term employment relationship. *The right career* is a bigger concept and may include several jobs, all at the same time or in sequence. It may include a series of jobs over time or it may be a composite career made up of several types of work. *The right work,* the biggest idea of the three, embraces both right jobs and right careers. It is about how we employ our talents in the world.

IS THIS BOOK FOR YOU?

This book is for job seekers of all kinds, whether the goal is a first job or a job to retire from, a part-time job, a factory job, or an executive job. It is for those who want to become more skillful at the business of finding a job. It is for those who want more effectiveness and less frustration in their search. It is for those who want to know what work is right—appropriate, suitable, most likely to be rewarding—and how to get it.

This is a book for people on *both* sides of the desk in any interviewing situation. Just as a book on winning tennis is written for players on both sides of the net, this book is intended to help anyone who will take time to read it and put its principles into practice, regardless of where they are in the game.

In this book the main perspective is that of the person seeking an interview, seeking a job, seeking a new career. But for every person like that there are people who seek benefits from granting an interview, who need to fill a job, or who want to find motivated career changers. These people, too, can become more effective by learning what is in this book.

After all, most interviewers have been and will be interviewees. Most who have jobs to fill have themselves been through the hiring process. Most who have work that needs to be done have themselves sought work. In a very real sense, then, all who seek greater personal effectiveness need to become more skillful at interviewing.

*It's no longer obligatory to
accept the next job which
comes along in the career
field you find yourself in
after school. The new American job game is on and you
are a player.*

Tom Jackson, *Guerrilla Tactics in the Job Market*

USING THIS BOOK

There are many, many ways to use this book. For instance:

- As a way to get started on your job hunt
- As an idea source at the beginning of your campaign
- To perk up a job hunt gone flat
- To heighten your knowledge of the skills, passions, and values you bring to your work
- To make your résumé more effective
- As a source for ideas on how to uncover job openings
- As a last-minute confidence builder and skills refresher before going into a big interview
- As a reminder of ways to ask for the job
- To understand what happened after an interview gone sour
- To learn how employers think about the hiring process
- To help your friend or relative get his or her dream job
- To become a better career counselor
- To improve the hiring process in your company, in your industry, and in the world about you

READING THIS BOOK

Just as there are many ways to use this book, there are many ways to read it. The book is roughly sequential in organization, with the ideas designed to flow from one to the next. The traditional approach of starting with the first page and reading right through to the last will work fine here.

But it is also fine to skip around, reading relevant topics selectively. Someone struggling to create a résumé, for instance, would get particular help in Chapter Eight, "Résumés and Other Door Openers," and someone with an interview the next morning would profit from rereading Chapter Fourteen, "Winning First Impressions." The first five chapters, with nine steps to knowing your right work, offer a simple system for self-knowledge that can be used at any time.

The Ultimate Interview can also be used as an exercise book. There are no commands designed to stop you in your tracks until you complete an assigned written task, and there are no blank pages with lines to write on. But there are suggestions made that can lead you to highly productive self-directed exercises.

Finally, this is a resource book, an aid station you can visit before an interview, just after one, or when you are at a loss about how to get the next one. Come back to the book for a reminder about how to do things better or for the one step you had forgotten. Use it as a support system to enable you to meet the next interviewer with an extra surge of confidence.

In short, this book contains everything you'll ever need to know about how to get the job you've always wanted. It tells how to know what work is right for you and how to get it, who to contact and how to approach them, and how to conduct a successful interview. On this subject it is exhaustive, covering every possible aspect of interviewing. It tells you how to change the interview from a barrier to your progress into a gateway to worklife success. Most importantly it tells you what you need to know to be the candidate who goes home happy, with the job offer in hand.

ONE Focusing

Nine Steps to Knowing What Work Is Right for You

1 WISHES: What work challenges do you want? What work conditions? What rewards?

2 EXPERIENCE: List every job you ever had—even as a kid! What does this tell you about what work is right for you now?

3 LIKES: In your work history, what are the jobs, activities, and achievements that satisfied you the most? What about today?

4 GIFTS: What skills, knowledge, and passion do you have to offer an employer?

5 VALUES: What do you value in your work? What purposes and practices are right for you, morally and ethically?

6 OPTIONS: What kinds of work are right for you? Realistically, what are your job options?

7 MONEY: How much do you want? How much do you need? How much do you expect to need three years from now?

8 PRIORITIES: What happens when you weigh, rank, and analyze your likes, gifts, values, and options?

9 FIVE FRIENDS: What do five of your closest friends think about what work is right for you? How can they help you get it?

CHAPTER ONE

DESIRE AND SUCCESS

CONSIDER life's basic questions: What is the meaning of it all? Where can I find happiness? What work is right for me? In pondering them, we discover that there are no final answers and that the tentative ones keep changing, sometimes day to day. But there can be fabulous value in asking the questions again and again.

The closer we come to our own individual truth in answering the third of these life questions, the more likely we are to be successful in our job hunt. The first five chapters of this book are here to move you toward that answer.

In this Focusing section, you will find nine steps to knowing what work is right for you. Read them, think about them, write about them. You can make them big steps or little steps, slow steps or fast steps. But if you take all nine, you will significantly increase your job-finding success.

As in love and in life, it begins with knowing what you want.

Those who study human behavior tell us that desire and fear are the two great motivators. Instinct and emotion are what move us to action, desire pulling us ahead and fear driving us from behind.

Everything we do can be traced to one or the other of these great motivators. The better we understand this, the more likely we are to create satisfying lives. The more we know about our own desires and our own fears, the better our chances for making the right choices.

In work, our choices are profoundly influenced by desire and fear. Sometimes one dominates, sometimes the other, but of the two, desire produces the most satisfactory long-term results—partly because desire, more than fear, leads to meaningful accomplishments; partly because desires reflect talents, experiences, and those inexpressible impulses that make each human being unique.

> *The desire accomplished is*
> *sweet to the soul.*
> Proverbs 13:19

For those committed to learning what work is right for them, the place to start is with desire. For those of us who want work that is appropriate to our talents, our experience, and our passions, the place to begin is with an understanding of what it is we want from life. Unless we are aiming for the right target, why even pick up the bow?

This is why the first of nine steps to knowing what work is right for us is about wishes. If one of your wishes is to know what kind of productive activity is most likely to be appropriate for you, then start now on these nine steps. They reflect the collective wisdom of authors, teachers, career counselors, and hundreds of ordinary people struggling with worklife issues. They offer you both insight and clarity.

No matter how sure you are about where you are going, your confidence will be raised and your job-finding effectiveness enhanced if you are clear about where you stand on each of these steps.

Step 1 **WISHES** On a plain sheet of paper, make three columns headed CHALLENGES, CONDITIONS, and REWARDS. Under the first head, write down all the things you would like to do in your work to help achieve the goals of those for whom you work or aspire to work—clients, customers, or people within an organization. Under the second head, write down all the conditions you wish for at work, especially the human and physical dimensions of your work environment. Under the third head, write the rewards you would like, both psychic and material.

> *Contrary to what you may have*
> *been taught, there is nothing*
> *frivolous or superficial about*
> *what you want.*
> Barbara Sher, *Wishcraft*

SAMPLE WISH LIST

CHALLENGES	*CONDITIONS*	*REWARDS*
Building sales	Stimulating people to work with	Acknowledgment for doing well
Improving customers service	Schedule my own time	Training on the job and off-site
Learning new technology	Clean, friendly office environment	Good salary, plus incentives
Leading work teams	Lots of activity	Promotions
Controlling costs		

Each of the three categories is important, and their sequence here is intentional. Challenges come first in any work and largely dictate the conditions. Rewards come at the end.

Challenges Some people are victims of challenges they did not intend to create for themselves: how to pay the rent or fix the car or correct a mistake at work or repair a troubled relationship. Other people pick their challenges, focusing on problems they would enjoy solving. You want to be in the second category.

What do you want to create? What do you want to produce? Are you interested in generating ideas and concepts? If so, list them. Are you interested in creating things—cabinets, houses, watercolors? Do you want to work with people to make things happen? If so, how? Do you want to lead people? To manage them?

What do you want to engage with each morning when you begin work? Where do you want to put your energy? What do you want to be responsible for? What will make you feel good at the end of the day or week, knowing you have accomplished it?

This is the toughest part of the wish list because most of us instinctively avoid challenges. As children we learn to be somewhere else when work assignments are passed out. Yet we need challenges, however old we are: to be challenged is to be alive. We need mountains to climb and problems to solve. Life can deliver us some awesome challenges, but if we think about what we truly want, we can also pick some of our own.

Conditions Where you want to contribute and with whom and for what purposes is also crucial to knowing what work is right for you. Do you want to work in the city or in the country? Put that on your list. Do you want to work near where you live now or in some other part of the world? What kind of physical surroundings do you want? List everything you can think of.

With whom do you want to work? What kinds of people? With what kinds of interests and values? Under what conditions and in what settings? With just a few people or with a lot? Do you want to be buying, selling, leading, following, operating as part of a team? Do you want to be friends with people at work, and socialize with them?

Finally, think about what purposes you want to work for? Are you passionate about the environment, about housing, about books, about making healthful food available? If so, this should be on your list.

> *Winning means getting what you want. Not what your father and mother wanted for you, not what you think you can realistically get in this world, but what you want—your wish, your fantasy, your dream.*
> Barbara Sher

Rewards   The last category on your wish list is rewards. What do you want in return for successfully meeting the challenges you choose under the conditions you would like? Think of psychic rewards like the feeling of a job well done and praise from coworkers and bosses. Think of accolades you would like. By whom would you be honored in your wildest fantasy?

Think of more tangible rewards. Would you like promotions? A nicer office or workspace? Money? If money is on your list, put down specific amounts for specific time periods. Would you like a salary or a bonus or some combination? Would you like to be on commission? Would you like money to come directly to you from satisfied customers? Would you like the pleasure of profits from a business you create?

Would you like to feel as though you are getting better at what you do? Would you like to keep on growing? Would you like training programs and study opportunities as a reward for your contributions at work? If so, list these under REWARDS, being as specific as you can.

COACHING TIP

To make your wish list richer and more complete, pretend that you are six years old and a genie has just risen out of an old lamp to offer you three wishes about work. What challenge would you most like? What work conditions? What rewards? Take your time. Think about it. Wishes do come true!

When you think you are finished listing all your wishes—for challenges, conditions, and rewards—take a moment to review what you have written. Sometimes the best comes last, so see if you can add three more items. Take a red marker and put a star in front of those items on your list that are most important to you. At the bottom of your list, write your best answer to the question: At this moment in time, knowing what I know now, what work is right for me?

Now go on to the next step.

Step 2 **EXPERIENCE** On as many sheets of paper as it takes, record your work experience. Start with the first job you had, whether you were paid for it or not, and show the dates you did the work, your title or job designation, and what activities and accomplishments were involved. Complete this listing in as much detail as you can provide right up to your present or most recent work.

This exercise is about success, something all of us have experienced. The best way to prepare for future career success is to acknowledge past successes. The way to do that is to record successful work experiences, in Step 2 on the path to knowing our right work.

> *Boast a little. Boast a lot. Who's going to see this document, besides you, God, and any twenty people that you choose to show it to?*
>
> Richard N. Bolles, *What Color Is Your Parachute?*

As you make this record, let yourself go. Boast a lot, as Richard Bolles advises those doing such exercises. This will free up achievements you may have forgotten and reveal patterns of achievement that may prove helpful in reaching conclusions on what work is right for you. Be willing to spend a lot of time with this exercise, and do so with the knowledge that this is some of the most valuable work a job seeker can do. Back up what you write with lots of concrete examples and figures—even if you have to look in your files or make some guesstimates.

This exercise will give you new, or forgotten, information about yourself. It will give you new inspiration, ideas for words to use about yourself, and it will add to your self-confidence. It will suggest jobs for the future and will also provide you with top-quality raw material for a résumé (which comes later). This is important because it will put you way ahead of those who start cold.

When this work history is finished, review it and add notes on points you may have missed. Take your time. Thoroughness pays big dividends here. Then write your best answer to the question: At this point in time, knowing what I know now, what is the right work for me?

"Nothing succeeds like success," goes the French proverb. As a contemporary job seeker, learn from your successes and mix what you learn with your desires for the future. Then notice how you find yourself going in the right direction.

▲

CHAPTER TWO

FOLLOW YOUR BLISS

"**W**HAT is your best advice to us?" Joseph Campbell was asked on his eightieth birthday. As an admiring audience of eight hundred listened intently, Campbell replied with a broad smile, "Follow your bliss."

Campbell was led to his passion for mythology by a boyhood interest in American Indians. At Columbia University and in Europe, his curiosity led him to explore diverse cultures. During the Depression, he spent five years in the full-time pursuit of great literature. As a professor at Sarah Lawrence College, he popularized the study of mythology, a subject that inspired him to the end of his life.

True leaders are always led.
Carl Jung

Go where your passion leads, Campbell told people again and again. Follow your zeal; pay attention to where life is leading you. Do not be distracted by what your father wants you to do or by the siren call of riches. If you are on the right path, *your* path, you will find everything you need. Including fulfillment, recognition, and money.

How do you know where your bliss lies? The best way is to look backward into your experience and notice what has given you pleasure in the past. This is step three on the path to knowing your right work.

Step 3 **LIKES** Go back to the work history you prepared for Step 2. With a yellow highlighter, mark the jobs, activities, and achievements you found particularly satisfying. Put a red star beside those you liked the most. On a separate sheet of paper, cluster the key ideas in groups and give each group a name.

Employers spend so much time on your past, as revealed by your résumé, your references, and job interviews, because a person's past is the best indicator of his or her future. People change slowly. What we did last month or last year tells a lot—not everything, but a lot—about what we will do in the coming months and years.

A look into your past is extremely valuable for outsiders who want to predict your future behavior, but it is even more valuable for you. If you want to know what will give you pleasure and fulfillment in the future, scrutinize your past. The better your self-understanding, the more likely you are to be an effective worker and a successful person.

> *Your interests, wishes, and happiness determine what you actually do well, more than your intelligence, aptitudes, or skills do.*
> Richard N. Bolles

The experience of vocational psychologists and personnel professionals suggests that what you like is an excellent indicator of what you will do well. The experience of Dick Bolles, who has worked with thousands of job seekers and career changers, suggests the same.

After you have done the yellow highlighting on your work history and added the red stars for the most important items and clustered the key ideas in groups you should have a clearer picture of where *your* bliss lies.

To get even more value from Step 3, try this. On another sheet of paper, again make three columns headed CHALLENGES, CONDITIONS, and REWARDS. Take what you have learned about your likes and put as many items as you can in each of the three columns. What challenges do you like most? What working conditions do you like most? What rewards do you like most?

Now go back and compare this to what you had for the same three columns in Step 1 and see if that suggests other items, things you may not have thought of or remembered. Add these to your list.

> *When I was growing up I really*
> *wanted to be somebody. Now I*
> *realize that I should have been*
> *more specific.*
> Lily Tomlin

Notice how the first three steps form a cohesive whole, a multi-dimensional look at you, what you want, where you have been, and what gives you joy. The fourth step builds from the first three but is a major leap forward, calling for your best creative thinking.

Step 4 **GIFTS** On a plain sheet of paper, make three columns headed SKILLS, KNOWLEDGE, and PASSION. Under SKILLS list your talents: what you are able to do. Under KNOWLEDGE list the topics and technical fields you know something about. Under PASSION list what you care about. These are your gifts.

To get the most value from Step 4, get lots and lots of ideas down and then weight and prioritize them. The more you have to draw from, the more likely it is that your priorities will be meaningful. Here is one way to do this.

Skills. Skills are represented by action words, like "reading" (what you are doing now), "understanding," and "integrating" (what you are doing now if this is making sense to you). Start by listing such basic skills. Then expand into more specific skills, like "reading financial reports" and "understanding human motivation." Go back to your work history to pick out skills listed there. Again, make them specific. List as many subcategories as you can. Under communicating, for instance, you might have "listening," "asking questions," "making connections," "rephrasing," "persuading," and more.

You should have lots of words by now, so it is important to organize your skills. Do this by putting a red star by those that are most important to you. You should have some that are the same or quite similar. These make up skill clusters. Each skill cluster should be given a name and these names listed at the bottom of the page, with the most important clusters first.

> As a human being you are en-
> dowed with, and have acquired,
> a large variety of personal and
> technical tools for dealing with
> the world around you.
>
>   Tom Jackson, *The Perfect Ré-
> sumé*

Knowledge. Your knowledge has grown through the use and de-
velopment of your skills. If you use your reading skill it could give
you knowledge of "espionage management," if you are a John le Carré
fan, or of "computer technology," if you are a devotee of PC trade
magazines. Some knowledge is gained by reading and study, some by
doing. Both kinds are important. A knowledge of Manhattan streets
could be significant, for instance, if you wanted to work as a tour
guide or taxicab driver in New York City.

As with skills, list as many areas of knowledge as you possibly
can, then put a red star by those that are most important to you.
Cluster these in categories that make sense to you and list the clusters
at the bottom of the page, with the most important first.

Passion. Passion moves us forward. It is the collection of interests,
motivations, and concerns that keeps us going. In this part of Step 4,
list the immediate sources of your passion, like "doing quality work"
and "making a contribution each day." Think about what motivates
you. Check back under REWARDS on the wish list you developed in
Step 1 for additional ideas on what you really care about.

Then list the larger sources of your passion, like "helping dys-
functional families" or "highway safety" or "world peace." Take time
to get down everything you care about, both close to home and far
out in the future.

Now put a red star by those that are most important to you. If
you see any clusters, give them a name and include them in a list at
the bottom of the page, with the most important first.

*In rapidly increasing numbers,
people are realizing that work
time lacking in satisfaction and
fulfillment is wasted time. You
don't have to do penance in
order to earn money.*

Jay Conrad Levinson, *Quit
Your Job*

Sample: One Person's GIFTS

SKILLS	KNOWLEDGE	PASSION

Communication
  listening
  talking
  writing
	Sales technique
	  prospecting
	  presenting
	  closing
	  follow-up
		Building things, like
		  work groups or
		  new programs

Problem Solving
  diagnosing
  brainstorming
  planning
	Computers
	  workstations
	  word processing
	  spread sheets
	  training
		Persuading people to
		  do what's right
		
		Producing high-qual-
		  ity work

Motivating
  explaining
  inspiring
	Psychology
	  motivation
	  human interactions	

Self-Management
  time planning
  prioritizing
  goal setting		

Leading
  making plans
  getting agreement
  follow-up		

All of us have glorious gifts. The challenge is to unwrap them, throw off the tissue and packaging under which they lie dormant, and bring them fully into use. The challenge is to bring our skills, and knowledge, and passion to the work we do, every day, every month, every year.

"Follow your desire as long as you live," wrote the Egyptian philosopher Ptahhotpe over four thousand years ago. The advice is still relevant. Sooner or later, we must stake our claim in the world. We must proclaim our own gifts and say this is where I've been, this is what I want, and this is what work is right for me.

▲

CHAPTER THREE

IDEALS AND OPTIONS

NOTHING shapes our lives more than what we value. Not fate, not circumstances, not childhood experience. If we want to know what work is right for us, we must know what we value.

> Everything we do, every decision we make and course of action we take, is based on our consciously or unconsciously held beliefs, attitudes, and values.
>
> Sidney B. Simon, *Values Clarification*

This becomes the next step on the road to the right work.

Step 5 VALUES On a plain sheet of paper, list what you value in your work. Start by reviewing the items shown below and then add your own. List everything you can think of that is important to you.

Although we live our lives by what we value, values are tough to sort out and tougher still to put into words. To help you see where you stand, some work-related values are described below.

▲ **Friendship.** How much do you value interacting with other people? How important to you are the human relationships in your work?

▲ **Achievement.** How much do you care about making

things happen? How important to you is a feeling of accomplishment at the end of the week or at the end of the year?

▲ **Power.** How much do you value being in control of projects at work? Do you like being responsible for who does what and who gets what and how the rewards are passed out?

▲ **Prestige.** How important is it to you that others think well of you? How strongly do you feel about the esteem that comes to you from your work?

▲ **Money.** How important to you is the amount of money you are paid? What is the relationship between the money you earn and how good you feel about your work? Step 7 considers money as a separate issue, but it also belongs on just about everyone's list of values.

▲ **Praise.** How important is it that others tell you that you are doing well? How much do you care about kind words?

▲ **Learning.** How significant to you is what you learn at work? How much do you value new knowledge and new skills and the process by which they are acquired?

▲ **Contribution.** How important is it to you that your work contributes to making this a better world? How strongly do you feel about global issues?

Working down this list may have suggested some other values that are important to you. If so, add these to the list you are developing for yourself.

Go back to Step 2 and look through your work experiences to see if other values suggest themselves to you. Keep asking yourself: What about this job or that achievement indicates what is important to me?

Go back to Step 3 and look through your likes list to get more clues on your values. The longer your list of values, the more likely you are to have an accurate picture when you assess the results.

COACHING TIP

Make a list of the people you most admire. Next to each name, write one or more things you admire about that person. Circle the words that are attributes you value. As you encounter new people in the coming days, add to your list.

Still on Step 3, make a list of your dislikes, the things you hated about jobs in your past. What does this tell you about what you value? Go one step further and make a list of the things you fear in work. Be brutally honest. What do you dread? What gives you a sick feeling in the pit of your stomach? What does this list tell you about what you value?

Semantics is not important here because values, standards, ideals, and beliefs often overlap. "Wearing nice clothes" is just as important to list as "smoke-free environment." What you want here is insight more than precise usage.

When you have listed every value you can think of, see if you can cluster several into one larger and more significant category. Now imagine that you have 100 points to distribute as a reflection of the relative importance of these values in your worklife. Go over your list and allocate the 100 points to the five to eight items that are most important to you. This step is critical because all values are not equal, and because of the crucial role values play in work choices.

> *Ideals are like the stars. We can not reach them but we profit by their presence.*
> John Le Carré

Like the stars, values guide those who pay attention to them. Like the stars they inspire us regardless of where we are on the path or how well the journey is going. However, unlike the stars, which are unreachable, we should try to attain and hold on to our values.

Now look one more time at your values list and ask yourself: What does this tell me about what work is right for me? Record your answer at the bottom of the list and go on to Step 6.

Step 6 **OPTIONS** Based on what you know now, list the kinds of work or jobs you think might be right for you. Do not worry at this point about availability or whether you are qualified. Rank the top five on the list, with 1 being the most attractive, 5 the least.

The premier career-counseling question is: What do you *think* you would like to do? Admittedly, not always an easy question to answer. Once when I replied that I really didn't know, the retort was, "Well, who should I ask?"

In fact, no one is better qualified to come up with job ideas than the person who is looking for work. Career counselors may help, and parents and friends usually have ideas. But the one who is going to live with the decision usually has the best instincts for producing the right answer.

> *Despite several decades of research, the most efficient way to predict vocational choice is simply to ask the person what he wants to be; our best devices do not exceed the predictive value of that method.*
> Dr. John Holland

Because developing options is one of the toughest parts of this whole process, you may want to try several approaches. Here are five of the best:

1 *Review the exercises, lists, and other notes you have made about your work.* Specifically, go back over the words and thoughts you generated in the first five steps of this process and see what job ideas you find. What were your answers when you asked yourself what work seemed right for you? What other answers occur to you now? List as many options as you can, no matter how outrageous they may seem. You can bring in reality later. One way to get these on paper is to take a large sheet of newsprint and put one job idea in the center and then see what grows out of it, connecting one idea to the other by lines and boxes in a mind-mapping exercise.

2 *List jobs or kinds of work done by people you know, and note which seem attractive to you.* You can take a piece here and a part there as

well as whole jobs. Start by reviewing family members, since this is work you are likely to know best, and then go on to friends. Think about the times when you have said to yourself, "Wow, I'd really like to be doing that!"

3   *Fantasize. Use your imagination to pick up clues from your unconscious mind. Listen to your impulses and instincts.*

▲ Close your eyes and imagine that it is five years in the future and you are leaving the house to go to work. See every detail of the commute, if there is one, and every specific about the work you do. At the end of this journey, return to the place where you live, open your eyes, and describe on paper what you have seen. This imaging exercise was developed working with college students in Florida, and I have used it with hundreds of clients in dozens of workshops. It works.

▲ Write a letter to someone you love and date it two years in the future. Begin by saying that you have found just the right work and then describe it. Tell what you are doing for whom and with whom. Include as much detail as you can muster. Toward the end, tell how this work makes you feel and then sign it "Love," and your name. This exercise comes from a Dick Bolles workshop and has worked beautifully for a number of my clients.

▲ Pretend that you have been given an assignment by your local newspaper to write the obituary for an important person: *you.* Write about your life in the third person, focusing particularly on what you have achieved in your worklife. When you are finished, look for clues about work options in your life *today.*

4   **Look in your newspaper, both in articles and in the want ads, for jobs or kinds of work that appeal to you.** Look in the Yellow Pages of your phone book under categories that interest you. Go to your library and ask for the Dictionary of Occupational Titles to see if you can find some ideas there. Look at books on job finding to see if they have other ideas.

5   **Go back to Step 3 and get your five most important likes.** List these, equally spaced, across the top of a page. Then go to Step 4 and get your five most important gifts. List these down the left side of the page, and draw lines to create a twenty-five-box grid. Fill as many boxes on the grid as you can with one or more job ideas. The beauty of this exercise, according to Tom Jackson, who developed it, is that you are creating job options directly from your own skills and interests.

> *You can use your worklife as an opportunity to continually express yourself in the world in a way which brings you a direct day-by-day experience of satisfaction and a good paycheck.*
>
> Tom Jackson, *Guerrilla Tactics In the Job Market*

William Hewlett, cofounder of Hewlett-Packard, talks about "inventions of opportunity," scientific discoveries that were totally unplanned. He encourages H-P researchers to be receptive to such opportunities, and I encourage you to do the same. You may find a job option where you least expect it. If you are open-minded, you may find exactly what you need next in your worklife. If you are ready for them, "options of opportunity" can be the best work options of all.

As you finish Step 6, stay open to other job possibilities. You will get additional ideas as you complete the steps in the path leading to work that is right for you. You will even get valuable ideas as you begin the interviewing process. Stay alert and you may be pleasantly surprised at where the journey ends.

▲

CHAPTER FOUR

MONEY AND HAPPINESS

IN his twenties, Joseph Campbell lived for five years on "nothing." He lived rent free in a converted chicken coop in Woodstock, New York, ate simply, and spent ten hours a day reading the classics. According to Campbell, it was one of the happiest times in his life.

For a host of reasons, such simple living is available to very few of us. But Campbell's experience is instructive to those of us who ponder the role of money in our lives and its relationship to happiness.

> *Money has become for us what sex was to an earlier genera-tion—difficult to face honestly and impossible to ignore.*
> Dr. Jacob Needleman

Thus, the next of the nine steps to knowing your right work:

Step 7 **MONEY** Make a list of what you actually spent last year, including taxes. Using the same expense categories, make a list of how much you *need* per year and beside that how much you *want* per year. Finally, estimate what you will need and what you would want three years from now.

Most of us are uncomfortable talking about money, especially the money we earn and the money we spend and the money we save. In our society, money is a major indicator of human worth and has enormous implications for our self-esteem. A lack of money stirs our primal fears of not being loved, of being abandoned, of not surviving. Little wonder money is hard to talk about!

The easiest way to deal with money is to deal with reality. What is actually happening? In the latest calendar year, how much did you spend on housing, in rent or mortgage payments? How much did you spend on food? On transportation? On clothes? On insurance? On travel and vacations? On education? On charitable giving? On taxes? On everything else? It will take some time to put these numbers together and in some cases you will have to estimate, but the result is worth the effort.

> *I have no quarrel with making money. The reason I deliberately put the word money into the title of this book is so that readers could be assured that part of my definition of a successful life involves having the means to provide for ourselves and those who depend on us.*
>
> Marsha Sinetar *Do What You Love, the Money Will Follow*

On a separate sheet of paper, list how much you need per year, right now, and how much you want. Need means what you can live on and want means what you would like to live on—with some left over for savings and gifts.

	NEED	*WANT*
Housing		
Food		
Transportation		
Clothes		
Insurance		
Travel & Vacations		
Education		
Charitable Giving		
Taxes		
Other Category		
Other Category		
Miscellaneous		
Total		

Now do a similar NEED/WANT list for three years from now. Forecasting is difficult, I know, especially when you're talking about the future. But do it anyway. This is your life we are talking about, your future, and your dreams.

What have you learned from this money exercise? Make notes on your sheet to record this. What does the issue of money say about what work is right for you? Record this also.

COACHING TIP

The figures you prepare for this step will help you when it comes time to agree with your new employer on compensation. Review them then and you will be a more confident negotiator.

Numbers are difficult, particularly when we are applying them to our lives, because we know instinctively that there is more to us than what can be measured. But numbers can be helpful, especially when combined with qualitative data and kept in perspective.

Determining your right work is not a numbers game, but numbers can help shape the answer.

Step 8 **PRIORITIES** Take your top three job options from Step 6 and list them across the top of a sheet of paper. List your top five values from Step 5 down the left-hand side. Take 10 points for each value and allocate them to the three options. Add down to see how your top three options measure up according to what you list as your values.

This is how your sheet might look:

	WORK OPTION A	WORK OPTION B	WORK OPTION C
Value #1	3	4	3
Value #2	2	6	2
Value #3	4	3	3
Value #4	1	5	3
Value #5	3	3	4
Total	13	21	15

In this example, Option B ranks highest, followed by Option C. At this point, you may want to shuffle your work options some. Do you want to try this analysis for one or two additional options? Is there one option that should be split into two or three parts so you can see how aspects of a job might measure up? Be flexible. Let this exercise work for you.

> *None of this makes sense until you prioritize. There is a vast difference between what's at the top of your list and what's at the bottom.*
>
> Richard N. Bolles
> (to workshop participants)

This step pulls the pieces together from the first seven. It invites you to get more focused about what you really want. Done thoughtfully, this step will clarify who you want to be and where you want to go with your worklife. For the job hunter whose calculations are shown below, for example, the best place to work with computers seems to be in a retail store, although selling to businesses also ranks high.

	SELLING COMPUTERS TO BUSINESSES	SELLING COMPUTERS IN A STORE	COMPUTER CONSULTING
Friendship	3	5	2
Independence	3	2	5
Learning	3	4	3
Money	4	4	2
Contributing	4	4	2
Total	17	19	14

If you want to get more sophisticated, go back to Step 5 and see how you weighted each value (how you allocated your 100 points—remember?) and factor those weightings into this table. But remember the law of misleading numbers: Estimates based on estimates are only as good as the most accurate estimate.

There is another useful analytical tool at this point and that is the T account. For each of your top three work options, take a separate sheet of paper and draw a line across the top, listing the option. Then draw a line down the middle forming a T. List the pluses for that job on the left side and the minuses on the right. Considering these pros and cons, which of the three now looks best to you? Note this on the bottom of the page.

This is also the time to bring in any test results. Have you taken the Strong-Campbell Interest Inventory or some comparable vocational testing instrument? What do those results say about your top three work options?

Now estimate how much you would earn from each of your top three options. Compare this to what you need and what you want, both now and in three years. What does this say about what work is right for you?

> *Do it! Money will come when*
> *you are doing the right thing.*
> Michael Phillips,
> *The Seven Laws of Money*

Money, and other numbers relating to units produced, hours worked, the square footage of your office, are only part of what work is all about. How you feel and your sense of being on the right track also count for a lot. The beauty of the advice from Michael Phillips is that it doesn't say how *much* money will come. You may discover that you are happier earning less money from work you love than getting loads of money from work that is killing you.

> *There are worlds without*
> *money . . . worlds of art, poetry,*
> *music, dance, sex—the essen-*
> *tials of human life.*
> Michael Phillips,
> *The Seven Laws of Money*

Enjoy the worlds without money while living in the world where money makes a big difference.

Ask yourself again, and keep asking yourself: What work is right for me? You have now completed eight of the nine steps on the path to knowing your right work. You are almost to the end . . . of the beginning of a successful job search.

FIVE FRIENDS

Finding the right work is a social process. We can think about it, read about it, and make plans on our own. But other people are invariably involved in our finding the work, getting the work, and doing the work. This is also true when we try to sort out what work is right for us, which is why the final step is to seek help from friends.

> *No man is wise enough by himself.*
>
> Titus Plautus, 200 B.C.

Step 9 **FRIENDS** Ask five friends what work they think is right for you. Encourage them to be candid. Ask for detail and clarification. Listen carefully. Integrate what you hear into your own thinking.

One of my jub hunts led me to an executive search professional named Charles Harreus. Charlie worked out of his home in the hills of a remote suburb, but I was desperate so I made the drive out to see him.

"I'm looking for a senior position in marketing management," I explained to Charlie, and recounted in great detail my experience and qualifications for such a job. When he finally found an opening, Charlie asked:

"Are you sure you want to be in business?"

I was shocked. Of course I wanted to be in business. That was what my background and education and experience all indicated. What else was there? But as I drove down the hill, disoriented and discouraged, I wondered what was behind that disturbing question.

What was Charlie Harreus hearing that I had missed? What did he see that I was blind to? What unconscious messages was I broadcasting? How did Charlie's impressions connect to the uncomfortable stirrings in my soul?

The encounter proved pivotal, for within a year I accepted a full-time academic position. I was hired on as chairman of the business department, true, and I used my management experience every day at the college where I worked, but I was no longer "in business."

Step 9 is about finding friends like Charlie Harreus. It is about finding people who care enough about you to be honest with you. It is about asking for help and then being skillful in listening for the answer.

Who should you ask? Family members often give excellent reflection: parents, siblings, spouses, children. But your family is biased, so you should also talk to teachers or people you know from school or work. To be sure you ask the most helpful people, make a list of ten friends or acquaintances—twenty is even better—and then put a red star beside the names of those you plan to approach.

What should you ask? The best question is the most basic: What work do you think is right for me? Try not to influence the answer by what you say beforehand. Tell your friends how much you value their candid opinion. Follow up by asking why? Be willing to hear the answer. Don't argue with what you are told.

> *A friend is a person with whom I may be sincere. Before him, I may think aloud.*
> Ralph Waldo Emerson

Like Emerson, value sincerity in your friends. Encourage candor. Ask for their best thoughts. And in return, give them your best thoughts, without rationalizations, exaggerations, masks, or muddle. Be honest with yourself and be willing to reveal what you discover.

Nan Keohane, president of Wellesley College, once told an interviewer:

> *The thing I hate most in this world is flattery. I don't want to be flattered. I want to be told what's going on and if people see things in a way that leads them to believe I've made a mistake or, even more important, am about to make a mistake, I want to know it.*

Discourage flattery. Encourage candid, expressive feedback at every opportunity.

> *Feedback is the breakfast of champions.*
> Dr. Kenneth Blanchard

When you have listened to five or more friends (and more is better), write down what you heard. Review what you have recorded and ask yourself again: What work is right for me?

With your new picture of what work is right, you are ready to start on the path to getting it. As you go, take along these five bits of friendly wisdom:

1   *No one gets it right the first time.* Do not expect to get the ultimate answer the first time you ask the question. Keep asking. Keep building on what you learn. Notice how you change over time and how that makes a difference in what is right for you.

> *Believe In Yourself.*
> The Wizard of Oz to Dorothy

2   *You are better than you think you are.* No matter how confident you are, there are some ways you sell yourself short. And most people in transition are not all that confident. Remember to believe in yourself and act as though you do. You do not have to be cocky; a little quiet confidence is sufficient.

3   *The more active you are, the more likely you are to get what you want.* Luck loves the active. So if you want good luck on the path to the right work, make that extra phone call, read that extra article, write that extra letter. Stay connected with your friends and prospective employers. Reach out. Initiate. Be active, active, active.

4   *Reality always wins.* Your only job is to get in touch with it. In the world of work, your job is to discover what is real about you and about the challenges you propose to engage. Keep looking for *your* reality.

5   *The search never ends.* You will find many answers, but the question remains and you will ask it again. Since you will be searching all your life, why not get really good at the process?

The reason five friends comes as the last of the nine steps on the path to discovering your right work is that friends are essential to what comes next. Treasure your friends. Appreciate them fully. How you do on getting work that is right for you has everything to do with how well you connect with the people who can help you make it happen.

TWO Getting Ready

▲

CHAPTER SIX

VISION POWER

*"You'd be perfect for this," my
friends would say. "You should
go up for this." And I would
say, "I know, actually. I am. I am
perfect for this."*

Paul Shaffer, before joining
David Letterman as Band-
leader

PAUL Shaffer liked "The David Letterman Show" before he ever
met the host.

"I saw some stuff that I thought was just fabulous," he remembers.
"They were very, very funny." An accomplished bandleader and key-
board artist, Shaffer learned about comedy in Las Vegas. He loved
Letterman's bizarre and biting sense of humor.

When interviews began for "Late Night with David Letterman"
Shaffer knew that the bandleader job "was a great spot for me. I just
had a feeling that it was. I just *knew.*"

Shaffer was invited by an agency to come speak to Letterman
about the show. "I wasn't confident they were going to hire me, but
I was quite confident that I was the right man for the job."

In that first meeting, Letterman asked, "What kind of band would
you do?"

"And I had my concept together," Shaffer recalls. "If I get the
job," he told Letterman, "my band will be the type of band you see
in a late-night lounge. Say you walked into the hippest lounge you
could think of—it's smoky and there's a four-piece band playing."

Letterman liked the idea.

Shaffer came in several more times and let more of his sense of humor show. "After about the third meeting, for whatever reason, they broke down and gave me the job."

Paul Shaffer had a vision of what it would be like to lead the four-piece band for David Letterman on a late-night show. Empowered by this vision, he got the job of his dreams—leading the World's Most Dangerous Band five nights a week.

In one form or another, the process that worked for Paul Shaffer is the one that works for us. Our path to the right work starts with a vision, is empowered by a vision, and comes back to a vision. Along that circular path there is lots of learning, negotiating, and deciding.

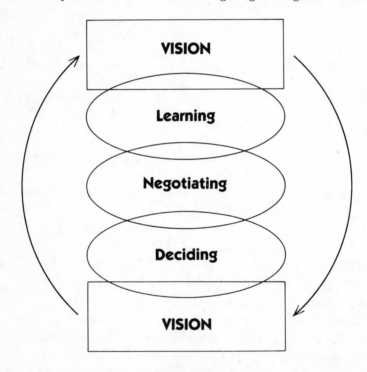

LEARNING

Life presents us with continuing opportunities to learn, and our worklife offers some of the richest of these opportunities. Curiosity, openness, and a willingness to see things differently all add value to our lives, particularly our worklives. The potential for learning is all about us as long as we draw breath.

In this book, for instance, the nine steps to knowing your right work are an opportunity for ongoing learning. Unlike a true-or-false quiz, the answers to the questions keep changing. Asked anew, they provide new insights and new information.

In the job-finding process, learning grows out of vision because successful action is preceded by reflection. In order to move ahead sensibly, we must first listen and ponder what we hear. Like an Indian scout, we find our way by looking carefully for signs of where the trail leads.

On the trail to dream jobs there are many kinds of learning:

▲ *Learning about ourselves,* our likes and aversions, our strengths and vulnerabilities. How hard are we willing to work? What motivates us? Where do we shine? Under what conditions are we most flexible and resilient? What is our vision, our dream job, and how is it changing?

▲ *Learning about those around us,* what works for them and what doesn't. What do we see in others that inspires us? What gives us courage to experiment? What do we see in others that we want to avoid in ourselves?

▲ *Learning about work,* about what is hot and what is not, about where we fit in and where we fade out. What part of the work we do are we best at? What parts are we inspired to get better at? What opportunities are coming our way from developing technology? What changes in the system work to our advantage? What's happening today to give us insights into tomorrow? Paul Shaffer learned what kind of music would work best for David Letterman's new show and he developed an appreciation for how the host liked to operate. What can we learn from Shaffer's experience?

> *Learn as though you were going to live forever. Live as though you were going to die tomorrow.*
>
> Johnny Wooden, UCLA basketball coach

One way to become a more successful job hunter is to keep a "Lessons Learned" journal. This can be any size, any quality, with lined pages or plain. It is for your use only, so don't worry about legibility or spelling. Focus instead on (1) what is happening on your job hunt, (2) what you are learning from what is happening, and (3) what you intend to do differently as a result. If you start your journal now you can use it to capture lessons learned as you go through this book.

NEGOTIATING

There is lots of give and take in job finding. There are compromises, trade-offs, and reassessments. The more knowledgeable we are about what is involved and the more skillful we become at negotiating for what we want, the better life works.

> *Like it or not, you are a negotiator. Negotiation is a fact of life ... Everyone negotiates something every day.*
>
> **Roger Fisher and William Ury,**
> *Getting to Yes*

In the process of finding a job, there is lots of back-and-forth communication about reaching agreements when not all values, interests, and perspectives are shared. For example:

▲ *Early in the process* there are negotiations about where to meet a friend to talk about work or how to arrange an interview with a high-potential employer.

▲ *Midway into the process* there are negotiations around job descriptions and job responsibilities. Employers flex and job seekers flex, each compromising as perceptions change and new information comes in.

▲ *Toward the end of the process* there is often negotiating about salary, incentives, workspace, responsibilities, and starting times. A fruitful time for negotiations is when the offer has been made but not yet accepted.

DECIDING

Life is made up of big and small commitments. Without them, nothing happens. Although we barely notice most of the decisions we make in the course of a day, major life decisions deserve special attention.

rience, is that there are many kinds of job interviews and many ways to get them.

COACHING TIP

Keep written records of each phone call and personal meeting on your job search. Record what happened and when. Update your files daily and keep them handy.

If you don't know where you are going you are liable to wind up somewhere else.
Yogi Berra

KINDS OF INTERVIEWS

On the path to the job of your dreams, you will find two kinds of interviews, those focused on exploration and those in which commitments are made.

Exploratory interviews are those in which you seek clarity, ideas, and focus: in a word, information. These can be a brief conversation in the hall or on the way to lunch. They can be by telephone as well as in person. They can be structured, prearranged interviews or they may be spontaneous and unplanned. These include informational interviews, where your primary goal is to collect data, but they also include qualifying interviews (Do they fit your qualifications? Do you fit theirs?) and screening interviews (Are they on your list of finalists? Are you on theirs?).

Commitment interviews are those in which decisions are made by you and by them. They include qualifying and screening interviews and can include informational interviews. Mainly they are final interviews in which agreements are reached about working conditions, rewards, and other conditions of employment. The climax of the commitment interview is the job offer.

Exploratory and commitment interviews overlap like two linked circles. Exploration and commitment are both ongoing activities and both can happen in the same meeting, as this diagram illustrates.

Exploratory   **Commitment**

Conversations in person or by phone with friends, counselors, and others in the know

Informational Interviews

Qualifying Interviews

Screening Interviews

Final Interviews with prospective partners, co-workers and bosses

Aim high. Expect that the search will produce quality candidates.

Lee Schweichler, *executive search professional, advising CEOs on how to identify management candidates*

If you have trouble knowing which kind of interview you want, read on. Your difficulty probably means that you are at a preliminary stage. The following suggestions will help you get the interviews needed to get you moving.

WHO TO APPROACH

Whatever kind of interview you want, the starting point is a list of people and companies you want to see. The best source of such names is friends—including those who helped you with the final step to knowing what work is right for you. Get ideas from these people and from everyone you encounter on your search. Keep asking, "Who else should I be talking to?"

Use other sources, too. The business section of your local newspaper lists companies that have moved and managers who have been promoted. These can suggest prospects. The classified ads list companies looking for people, some doing work like you want to do. The *Inc.* magazine list of the five hundred fastest growing companies may include businesses in your area. Trade directories list companies and people in those companies, all of whom can be prospects. And don't forget the Yellow Pages in the phone book, which can be an excellent source for ideas.

FACE-TO-FACE

How do you get an interview? The most effective way is in person, face-to-face. Getting in front of the person you want to ask for an interview can be time-consuming and difficult, but percentagewise no approach has a higher success rate. There are many, many variations on the in-person approach, some of which are:

▲ Go to the workplace of the person you want to see and ask politely but directly for a chance to talk. (This works better with middle managers and smaller companies, where you are less likely to encounter unfriendly gatekeepers.)

▲ Go to the workplace of the person you want to see and inquire about the best way to set up a meeting.

▲ Go to the workplace of the person you want to see and get to know someone else there who might help you get the interview you want.

> *After the final no there comes a yes. And on that yes all the world depends.*
> **Wallace Stevens**

▲ Better yet, call a friend who might know someone who works there and ask for an introduction. Research has shown that with seven phone calls you or I can reach anyone in the country, if we know the city where they live and keep focusing in with each call. Seven phone calls to reach anyone in the United States! For someone in your own area, it should take only three or four calls.

▲ Attend a trade association lunch or dinner meeting and meet people who are hiring people who do the work you want to do. Insurance underwriters, financial planners, corporate trainers, and hundreds of others have regular professional meetings. Most welcome visitors. All offer chances to meet people you might interview.

▲ Take a course in your field. Talk to the instructor and other students about job openings, the best companies to work for, and what it's like to work there. Use the fact that you're taking the course as one more reason for a prospective employer to interview you.

▲ Go visit your target company in the holiday spirit: dress in red and give away Valentine candies on February 14 or go in green with shamrocks on St. Patrick's Day. One Halloween I went to work dressed as a cowboy, because the client I was having lunch with said he was coming in costume. When I realized that my outfit was producing lots of smiles, I went after lunch to a company where I had been trying to see the president for six months . . . and got ten minutes with him.

▲ Go to a temp agency and see if they can get you an assignment at the company where you would like to work. You want to work as a manager? A recent *Wall Street Journal* article described The Corporate Staff, an agency in San Francisco that places executives in temporary assignments. Perhaps there is something like this near you.

> *Put the word out on the grapevine—at your professional associations, your clubs, with your friends and business acquaintances.*
>
> Martin John Yate, *Hiring the Best* (advising those who hire people)

▲ As a variation on the temp idea, arrange to work as a volunteer at the company where you hope to be interviewed.

▲ As a further variation, go to a company that provides singing telegrams (look under "Singing" in the Yellow Pages) and ask for assignments at the kinds of companies where you would like to get interviews.

▲ If you are in school, ask to interview a key person at your target company as part of a term paper assignment.

▲ If you are not in school, ask for such an interview so you can write an article on that person for your club news letter or the local paper.

▲ Arrange to present an award to the person you want to approach for an interview. Few people can say no to such an honor, so if you can arrange this through a club you belong to, and if the award is genuine and sincerely meant, you will almost always succeed with this strategy.

▲ As a variation on the award idea, invite the person you want to meet to come and speak before your club or service group. This is how I first met Caspar Weinberger, who, upon accepting the invitation, suggested that I come to his office to discuss the topic of his talk.

▲ You can even pay money for an interview, as I once did to get fifty minutes with a psychiatrist who had had a book published by a company I wanted to approach.

If some of these ideas seem outrageous, even preposterous to you, good. They are designed to stimulate your creativity and get you thinking about new ways to get the interviews you want. Be creative. Take some risks. Explore the boundaries of preposterousness in your life. Expand the limits of what you are willing to do to get what you want.

TELEPHONE POWER

If you cannot get an in-person interview, use the phone, where at least your voice is working for you. The telephone does not give you as much data as a face-to-face contact but it is faster and works best when you want to reach a number of people or need to make repeat contacts.

The secret of getting interviews over the telephone is to stay focused on your purpose: getting a face-to-face interview. You want to collect basic information—does the company seem like a good prospect for you, for example, and are you asking for the right person—but you do not want to be interviewed over the phone.

When you encounter a gatekeeper-secretary, try to have a name to give: "Mr. Jones, from the Jones Company, suggested that I call."

Secretaries respect power, and using the name of a third party will empower you in this situation.

COACHING TIP

If someone has agreed to call you back and you have not heard within three days, assume that they have misplaced your phone number and call again. This actually may have happened—it sometimes does!—and even if it didn't, your attitude of helpfulness will make the call go better.

Your goal on the telephone is to agree on a time to come for an interview, however informal. If that is inappropriate, ask if you could call back in a week or if there is someone else in the organization you should ask to see. If you still do not have a yes answer, ask for suggestions of other companies to see.

To add immediacy to your request for an interview use fax, modem, car phone, video phone, or other advanced communication forms—especially when the job you seek involves aggressive marketing of leading-edge technology. If you are in Hong Kong or Paris when you make your request, so much the better. Back up your request with an overnight letter sent by Express Mail, Federal Express or—if you are abroad—DHL.

Try secondary sources for job interviews, too, such as:

▲ Personnel agencies and executive search firms. While not as productive as direct approaches to employers, those who help businesses find employees are a good source of leads and valuable information. Use them to fill spaces in your job-hunt schedule.

▲ The placement office at your college or university. Even if you didn't graduate you might get job leads or valuable career counseling.

▲ Newsletter editors. For the industries that interest you, ask who is hiring and who to contact there. See if you can use the editor's name in asking for an interview.

▲ The friends, relatives, contacts, classmates, former bosses and ex-clients who are the core of your job-hunt support network.

To get faster results and instant feedback, use direct contact whenever you can. As an alternative or as backup, put it on paper. The written word is the most used (and most overused) way to get interviews, perhaps because it seems safest: no one was ever rejected by a mailbox or fax machine. There are, however, wonderful ways to use words on paper to advance your job hunt. All are described in the next chapter.

Your plan for getting interviews will probably include several approaches. Find the right balance, the most effective approaches for you. Find what works and reach out. Like a skillful coach, use a combination of approaches: personal contact followed by a letter reinforced by a phone call. Or whatever fits the situation. Experiment. Persevere. Be creative. Even outrageous.

A WALK IN THE PARK

Where should your interview be? Anywhere is the right place for an interview if you can talk, even for a few minutes, without distraction.

Most job interviews are held in offices or conference rooms, but you can also meet at a fitness club or tennis court. Some interviews are held in a frequent-flyer lounge at the airport, and one executive I know holds at least one flying interview with serious candidates, in order to see them away from the office, and to save time. You can meet over lunch or after a service club meeting or at a trade show. You can have a job interview while jogging or walking in the park.

FLEXIBILITY

"Steve and I decided to take a walk through Central Park," writes John Sculley in describing his sixth interview with Steve Jobs in the series that led to his becoming president of Apple Computers. Jobs and Sculley walked around the lake and up to the Metropolitan Museum of Art, where an important part of the conversation took place before an exhibit of Greco-Roman sculpture. Then they walked down through Central Park to Forty-ninth Street where Jobs led them to a record store and a conversation about music. Next it was an apartment building where Jobs was thinking of buying the penthouse suite. Three hours later, still walking, they headed back to Jobs' hotel.

Sculley talked to other executives at Apple out in California before deciding to leave Pepsi, and each of those interviews was essential.

Like links in a chain, each was part of the final result. Added one link at a time, each interview contributed a critical part to the completed whole, to Sculley's eventually accepting one of the top high-tech jobs in the world.

You too may have several interviews in your job search, and they may take place in more than one location. To find the success you seek, be persistent in asking for interviews, be flexible about where you will meet, and, one link at a time, keep building the chain.

▲

CHAPTER EIGHT

RÉSUMÉS AND OTHER
DOOR OPENERS

PAUL Hartzell began his worklife as a baseball player. Following graduation from Lehigh, Hartzell played for the California Angels, and later for the Twins, Orioles, and Brewers. Over six years, he pitched more than seven hundred innings of major league baseball.

When the time came to leave baseball, Hartzell was ready. As a player, he stayed in touch with a college alumnus who had gone into the securities field. As a result, Hartzell was offered a position as an account executive in the national firm where his friend was a manager, making a smooth transition into business.

Four years later, that job led to the position of Vice President of Sales for a major financial printer. Again, the people Hartzell knew were his biggest supporters.

Three years and many successes into this job, Hartzell had a phone call from the regional vice president of a much larger company doing financial printing internationally. A customer, it turned out, had given him Hartzell's name. "I've been in this business twenty-five years," said the voice on the other end of the line, "and this is the first time an investment banker has called me to recommend a sales guy."

That phone call led to interviews, some intense negotiating, and a job offer.

At age thirty-four, Hartzell has a new employer, a job with bright prospects, and a compensation package well into six figures. He manages a staff of twelve and is responsible for sales and production in a major metropolitan area. Hartzell's career opportunities came through the people he knew and stayed in touch with.

> ## COACHING TIP
>
> Make a list of people who might be helpful in your job search. Go over the list a second time and add names you had missed, names of people who do similar work to those on the list, names of people who might know those on the list. Lee Schweichler, who advises executives on how to hire, tells them to contact attorneys, accountants, bankers, and venture capitalists when looking for prospects. If you have contacts in those categories, add their names to your list.

Do you doubt the importance of contacts? According to a 1989 survey of 4500 employed people (by the National Center for Career Strategies), *70 percent found their jobs through networking and personal contacts.* Ads did it for 14 percent and executive search firms for 11 percent. Only 5 percent got jobs by mailing résumés.

In the business of finding the right work, nothing is so overrated as a good résumé. Self-knowledge, a network of friends, and an effective interview are all more important than the most impeccable résumé.

> *The closest a person ever gets to perfection is when they write a résumé*
>
> Robin Bradford, CEO, Bradford Personnel

Why then is the résumé so overrated?

Perhaps it is because it is a popular tool among the educated, many of whom have labored four years in order to be able to list the name of some institution of higher learning, followed by B.A. or B.S. Perhaps it is because the résumé is safe: We can put enormous time and energy into its preparation and then blame the postal service or an inept personnel manager if we do not get the response we want. Or perhaps it is because the résumé does have some valuable uses—even if these are not the uses for which the résumé has earned its main reputation.

RÉSUMÉ POWER

On the path to the ultimate interview it is essential to understand what the résumé is good for . . . and what it is not good for. The résumé is overrated and not very good for:

▲ *Getting interviews.* Contrary to popular belief, the résumé is not very good for getting interviews. In fact, a study from *Iron Age* magazine found that to get one job took an average of 1470 résumés—which may understate the problem. This means lots of wasted postage but, even worse, lots of wasted opportunity. The fact is that it's the people who know how to get interviews who are offered jobs while the résumés of equally qualified but less assertive people languish in a pile on someone's desk. A strong cover letter greatly improves the effectiveness of a résumé, but face-to-face and telephone requests are still much more likely to get results.

> *The most important thing you should know about résumés is that they are like mirrors in a funhouse: they offer a distorted image of reality whose main function is to deceive the eye.*
> Martin John Yate, *Hiring the Best*

▲ *Telling who you are.* Even though this is the ostensible purpose of the résumé, there are better ways to achieve the same purpose. The problem is the cereal-box syndrome: most résumés are designed for mass consumption, like a package of corn flakes, and not everyone likes corn flakes. You went to Ohio State? Maybe the person you want to see is a Michigan fan. You got your first job in 1952? Maybe this employer prefers twenty-year-olds. There is a time to handle objections like these, but it is not in the résumé. What you want is an interview, and what you want the prospective employer to have is just enough information about you to be motivated to go to that stage.

Here are five purposes that the résumé does fill—wonderfully:

▲ *Developing self-knowledge:* A thorough audit of your successes, skills, and passions (of the kind required in preparing a strong résumé) is invaluable in the entire job-search process and far more important than any single piece of paper. Knowing about yourself means knowing how you can be most effective at work.

▲ *Providing background.* Paul Hartzell's opening statement in his résumé: "Highly successful in dealing with senior management of major West Coast companies" summarized his main strength. He then gave his earnings for the past two years to illustrate the point. A marketing executive began her résumé:

DYNAMIC

MOTIVATED

POSITIVE

LADY

When used to provide background information and reinforce the truth about you, the résumé can be a powerful tool.

▲ *Creating and sustaining support networks.* A well-done résumé tells friends, family, various professionals, and even prospective employers what they need to know to help you. This is invaluable. Make sure such people have your résumé and that they can tell just by glancing at it how to reach you. Make sure they know what you want: "Trainee in Real Estate Property Management," for example, is a job objective people can understand and support.

▲ *Exchanging like a business card.* The business card is a traditional way of communicating over a support network. The résumé can function as an expanded version, offering more information. Used with discrimination and delivered with a smile, the résumé can do much more for you than a business card.

> *Fortunately, perhaps, there is no necessary connection between a résumé's quality and that of the candidate.*
>
> Martin John Yate, *Hiring the Best*

▲ *Saving your place in the applicant pool.* Some employers say they will consider *only* applicants who submit résumés. While they don't always mean this, be sure they have your résumé in their hands. As with the lottery, you don't have a chance if you don't buy a ticket. Like the lottery, however, the odds are long for hitting a big payoff if all they have is your résumé.

When combined with other job-getting strategies, résumés can be highly effective. Take Kathleen Snipes, who wanted a summer job in public relations, which was her major at Washington State University. During Christmas break she started telling people about her dream of working for the leading public relations firm in the city. One who listened was a man who, two days after talking with Kathleen, happened to meet a food technologist for that agency. The technologist knew the vice president running the summer intern program and was willing to help Kathleen get her job.

Three phone calls later, armed with a revised résumé targeted to the public relations firm, Kathleen got the interview and was on her way to the job she wanted. Contacts, phone calls, and effective written communications all figured in her success.

"No one ever took me seriously before," Kathleen admitted. "I can see now that if I take myself seriously, others will too."

BUSINESS LETTERS

The best written approach to getting interviews is a business letter. This is a format business people are used to and respond to.

> *I am much more impressed if a job seeker addresses a letter to me personally; these are the people I am going to see.*
> **Bank Vice President**

As with any business letter, it is essential to know whom to address. If you are looking for a job in sales, it is probably the sales manager. If you seek a job in finance, it is probably the chief financial officer. In writing such letters, it is better to address someone high in the organization rather then someone lower down. Correspondence passed down carries more clout than that passed up.

It is also essential to have extensive, pertinent, and up-to-date information about the company. What kinds of products and services does it offer, and how could you help make them better? The more information you have about the company, the better your letter will be.

The interview request letter has three essential parts:

▲ *The opening,* which tells who you are and why you are interested in this company.

▲ *The benefit,* which tells how your skills, knowledge, and passion could help the company be more successful.

▲ *The close,* which asks for an interview and promises a follow-up call.

Here is how such a letter might look:

Your home address
City, state, & zip
Your phone number
Today's date

Ms./Mr. Full name, title
Correct company name
Correct address

Dear _____:

At last week's computer show, I was impressed with what I heard about plans for expansion from several of your salespeople as well as from two of your customers. As a recent marketing graduate of State, and as a longtime admirer of your products, I am writing to see if there is a way I might contribute to your growth.

In addition to my sales and marketing classes at State, I have worked summers and weekends in a computer store, where my sales have consistently been 50 percent higher than those of any other part-time employee. My courses in computer programming at State have familiarized me with your equipment. My enthusiasm about the future of small computers would, I believe, put me in a unique position to be successful in selling your products and services.

I would like very much to discuss this with you in person. I will phone your office in the next several days to see if a meeting can be arranged.

Sincerely,

Your full name

Your immediate goal is to provide enough information to get an interview but not so much information that you risk being rejected without ever showing your face.

One of the best jobs I ever had, as chief marketing officer of a food company, came as a result of a letter just like the one above. When the hiring process was complete and I had agreed with my new boss, the president, on a starting date, I realized with a shock that I had never given him a résumé. What I had given him, in the course of several interviews, was everything he needed to make a decision. You should think that way, too.

CREATIVE ALTERNATIVES

Beyond letters and résumés there are many creative alternatives for using the written word in getting interviews. Consider these:

▲ *Make a poster,* like the one I saw recently with a big photo of a nice-looking man and the words, "BREAKING NEWS! ———— available for a job in broadcasting. Call (Los Angeles number) or (San Francisco number)." Your local speedy print shop can help.

▲ *Create a mini-résumé,* using the same principle as the poster but going small, say 5½ by 8½ inches or 3 by 5 inches, and including only the information you think might be relevant to getting an interview. Again, ask for help at your speedy print shop.

▲ *Have someone produce a video of you* dressed for an interview and telling the viewer about your achievements and strengths. "Video Production Services" in the Yellow Pages lists numbers to call for this service and might lead you to someone experienced in the visual approach to getting job interviews.

▲ *Reproduce a sketch or painting* of your own creation, as a way of visually communicating your talents to interested parties.

▲ *Reproduce an article you wrote,* demonstrating your competence in a relevant area (which is more important than whether you wrote the article for a national magazine or for your club newsletter).

▲ *Reproduce a glowing recommendation letter or article* about your skills and send it with a short note asking for an interview and telling how you can be reached.

> *We must learn to balance the*
> *material wonders of technology*
> *with the spiritual demands of*
> *our human nature.*
>
> John Naisbitt, *Megatrends*

▲ *Enhance any of these with a brief handwritten note,* adding your personal touch in a high-tech world. Write as you would talk, not as you would have your words carved in stone. Use colloquial phrases rather than business clichés. Verbs like "create," "build," and "manage," have more impact than hackneyed phrases like "in response to your recent ad" or "according to trade sources."

Be willing to ask for what you want more than once in more than one way. Be willing to be unorthodox in ways that will reveal yourself to people you care about. However, stay sensitive to those who are put off by nonconformity, especially established people in established companies. Know when to use a strong résumé as one of the many door openers at your disposal.

Remember the words of Rear Admiral Grace Hopper, U.S. Navy, retired, who, when asked on national television about her successful career, said, "Big rewards go to those who take big risks. A ship in port is not doing what a ship is intended to do."

CHAPTER NINE

EVERYTHING YOU NEED TO KNOW BEFORE AN INTERVIEW

"LET me tell you about how to get hired," the sales manager for a chemical company said to me recently. "This really happened.

"I was looking for a new salesperson and had interviewed a lot of candidates, without much success, when in comes this guy, in his early twenties, confident as hell, and wearing a $600 suit. He came recommended by the vice president of sales. How that happened, I don't know, but I do know he wasn't related.

"He's an impressive guy, and before long we're talking about specifics. I describe an open territory about three hundred miles from here, and he asks, polite as can be, 'Isn't it true that there's a territory open right here in the area?'

"Well, yes, I acknowledge that there is and, though we usually give those territories to more experienced people, we could probably make an exception.

"Next I mention the company car, a Chevrolet. 'Isn't it true that some of your field salespeople drive Oldsmobiles?' he asks, again very politely.

"Once again I admit that, yes, he's right. By this time, I'm wondering where he learned so much about us, so I ask him point-blank. 'I talked with three of your salespeople,' he tells me, 'and two of your customers.' I tell you, I was impressed.

"Then we get into money, and I tell him that the top of the range for his position is $45,000. He's quiet for a minute, and then says that he needs $55,000 . . . which was more than I was making at the time."

What happened?

"We hired the guy and gave him the territory and the car he wanted and $50,000 to start. I got a raise and a hell of a lesson in the value of having good information when you walk into a job interview."

> *The interview is a measured and ritualistic mating dance—it should have all the appearances of a relaxed conversation and produce as much information as an FBI dossier.*
>
> Martin John Yate, *Hiring the Best*

COLLECTING INFORMATION

In collecting information that leads to this kind of success story, start with sources that are available to everyone: newspapers, magazines, and reference books at the local library. Daily newspapers almost always have a business section, and many cities now have a newspaper covering just local business. Newsstands and libraries now have dozens of magazines with information on business in general and on specific companies. At larger libraries, you can also find financial data on many companies in reference books published by Moody's, Standard & Poor's, or Dun & Bradstreet.

If you let friends know of your information search you will be amazed at the clippings, photocopies of articles, and other snippets that come your way.

> *Have you ever thrown a stone in a lake and watched the circles of water grow wider and wider? A network of contacts expands in much the same way.*
>
> Ellen Wallach, *The Job Search Companion*

Begin with your friends to start making connections with those who work for the companies you would like interviews with. Who do they know in the company? Would it be OK to call? Who do they know that knows somebody who works there? Make the effort to pursue these leads and connect.

Not long ago, I tracked down two people who live in my area as preparation for a meeting with the president of a San Diego company. I wanted to meet them because of the work they were doing with the company, and I located them through my own perseverance and help from friends. In the process, I spent time on the phone and paid for some gas and a glass of wine. But when I flew in for that interview with the president I knew a great deal about his company, its people, its prospects, its pluses and its minuses. The interview turned out as I hoped; I know, in large part, because of the extra effort I put into preparation.

> *One time a candidate came in here, after being told that we don't do interviews, and gave me a ten-minute speech. When he took a breath, I interrupted to ask if he had any questions. He had none.*
>
> Admissions Director, Stanford Business School

KINDS OF INFORMATION

Here are the kinds of information to look for:

▲ *About the industry:* What's new in the industry? What are the trends? What are the implications of international competition? What about competition just down the street? If you want to work for IBM, read up on Apple. If you want to work for Avis, learn about Hertz. If you want to work for a cleaning service, find out about the others in town.

▲ *About the company:* What's happening in the company according to newspaper and magazine reports? What's happening according to financial reports (which most listed companies will give you for the price of a phone call to their shareholder relations department)? What's happening according to people who work there or know those who do? See what you can learn about challenges facing the company. See what you can learn about working conditions, about pay, about benefits.

> *Generally, today's candidates go into the interview uninformed. They are usually missing big pieces of data that could help them be more successful.*
>
> Tom Day, Executive Search Professional

▲ *About the people:* What can you discover about the people you might be working for or with? Where do they come from? What are their experiences? What can you learn about their strengths and weaknesses (as individuals and collectively)?

Not long ago, a recent college graduate walked into my office seeking information about a local entrepreneur I had mentioned in a radio interview. "Tell me all about him," this job seeker said to me, "and what I need to do to get work there." I told him all I knew, and he left my office better prepared for the interview he sought.

Imagine that you are collecting information as a school assignment and that the day of the interview you will be given a quiz: (1) describe the industry in which this company competes, (2) describe the company, its challenges, its policies, and its competitors, and (3) describe the people for whom and with whom you would be working.

SELF-KNOWLEDGE

Finally, review one last category of information: what you know about yourself. Review what you learned in going through the nine steps to knowing your right work. Ask again: What is my purpose and what are my goals? What are my talents and which do I most want to use in my work? What do I know and what do I get excited about? What specific successes can I cite to illustrate all this?

The more you know about the company, about the industry, about yourself, the better you will do.

A newspaper editor I know remembers the days when he was doing a lot of hiring. People would come into his office with an almost total lack of knowledge about the newspaper and ask questions that could have been answered with five minutes of preinterview research. He remembers wanting to say, "Here's a quarter; go down to the newsrack on the corner and read our paper. *Then* come back to talk with me."

Do your research. Get the facts. Be fully informed. Spend the quarter *before* the interview.

▲

CHAPTER TEN

PREPARATION, PRACTICE, AND PURPOSE

W HEN John F. Kennedy gave his acceptance speech at the 1960 Democratic Convention, he held one hand behind his back the entire time. Was this a power posture modeled after the Emperor Napoleon? Did he have his fingers crossed?

No. The future President of the United States, one of the great orators of our time, held his hand behind his back because it was bleeding. And it was bleeding because he had been so nervous before the speech that he had chewed his fingernails down past the quick.

Nervousness before a speech or interview is natural. Everyone has some, and that's good because it helps us perform at our best. But too much is liable to detract from our performance or leave us with bleeding cuticles.

How do we find just the right balance between alertness and nervousness? It is all in what we do to prepare, from the moment the date is set until the moment it arrives.

BEFORE THE INTERVIEW

Preparation starts at the outset of our quest for the job offer. It begins in earnest with the first interviews leading up to that event. Preparation is important in exploratory interviews and even more so in commitment interviews.

In anticipation of his visit, I had prepared videotapes of television commercials from the Pepsi Generation and Pepsi Challenge campaigns.

John Sculley, on his fourth meeting with Steve Jobs

John Sculley did not even want to leave Pepsi-Cola when he made a videotape for his meeting with Steve Jobs, but he was well prepared anyway. He knew the value of having a new career option even if he decided not to make a change. He knew that successful connections sometimes produce unexpected and wonderful results.

"That's just how we want it," Jobs said enthusiastically when he saw the Pepsi commercials. "We want to have the very best advertising at Apple, the highest quality possible." What could have made it more clear that John Sculley was the person to deliver just what Apple wanted?

Prepare well for interviews. Find your own equivalent of John Sculley's video and then learn from each experience. Remember that each interview at each stage in the process is practice for those at the next stage.

There are also ways, at every stage, to rehearse before actually going into the interview. Find a roommate, spouse, or friend and have them ask you some of the questions that will come up along the way: Why are you here? What are you best at and why? What are your qualifications for the kind of work we are talking about here? What have you learned from your work experience? Why are you making a change now? You can think of more, no doubt, and so can the people you rehearse with.

For more ideas, look at the questions in the Interview Guide at the back of this book. The president of a $70-million-a-year company, a client of mine, recently used them in preparing for an interview: his wife asked the questions and videotaped the responses.

You can also have someone scrutinize your résumé and ask you questions about it. What is the main message? Where are the soft spots? Where are the gaps?

There are several important benefits to be gained from such practice:

▲ It refines and sharpens your answers to basic interview questions.

▲ It helps prepare you for the unexpected questions—and gives you the poise and confidence to answer such questions.

▲ It increases your self-assurance.

▲ It strengthens your total interview performance.

▲ And ultimately, it ensures that you engage your talent and passion in work that is right for you.

If you are keeping a "Lessons Learned" journal, and I hope you are, now is a good time to record your impressions. You will be amazed at how writing will clarify your thoughts and goals. Putting them down on paper is a great way to define your current situation and free up your mind to go on to meet new challenges.

> In a two-month job search I filled a hundred pages in my journal. I had too many options and it helped me see the light at the end of the tunnel. I called my journal "Now What?"
>
> Mark Agnew, president of a company employing 80 people

PRACTICE, PRACTICE, PRACTICE

If you do not have a friend to practice with, get three-by-five-inch index cards and write out some of the interview questions from this chapter or elsewhere in this book. Put yourself in the interviewer's position. What kinds of questions would *you* ask an applicant for this job? What would *you* be looking for? Write down all the questions you can think of, particularly the ones you personally would find most difficult to answer. Then practice answering them, using a tape player to record what you say. Listen to your answers and make notes on how to make them more precise and effective. Repeat the process until you are completely comfortable with what you hear, assured that you are presenting yourself at your best.

The next step is to practice asking the questions *you* want to put to the interviewer: What different kinds of work are done here? What kinds of people do best here? What kind of challenges are most important in this company right now? Where is the company heading? And many more.

> *When looking for a job, even
> the most experienced manager
> has given up the power and
> control he had on the other
> side of the desk. He is un-
> trained for the job-hunting ex-
> perience.*
>
> Tom Day, Executive Search
> Professional

This step, too, is best done with a friend. In asking questions, start with those that are simple and nonthreatening and move toward those that are more complex and sensitive. Your purpose is to demonstrate genuine interest, build trust, and bring out the kind of information needed for both sides to make the right decision. This is more easily accomplished in qualifying and informational interviews and more of a challenge in commitment interviews. Whatever the stage, however, it is imperative that you become a skillful asker of questions.

> *If I have an author on and I read
> his book ahead of time, I feel
> terrible. I lose my curiosity.*
>
> Larry King, Radio Personality

Is there ever a time not to prepare? Only when you're as experienced at interviewing as Larry King, who knows the value of preparation and knows what kind of preparation is right for him. Preparation increases control, and control is something Larry King has in abundance as a result of his vast experience, international reputation, and gift for gab. The rest of us need to read the book ahead of time.

No one is totally prepared for every event in life—without uncertainty, where would the challenge be?—but we all need to learn our right levels of preparation and make the time to make it happen.

One important reason why Larry King is exciting to listen to is the way he openly expresses his curiosity. He stimulates his listeners with that electric, insatiable curiosity and with the range and depth of his informed mind. Job seekers bringing that kind of experience, preparation, and searching intelligence to an interview can create surprise twists and intriguing nuances. And that could mean stimulating discoveries and unexpected results for those on both sides of the desk.

▲

CHAPTER ELEVEN

DRESS FOR SUCCESS

"I always figure," a personnel executive once told me, "that they'll never look any better than the day they walk in for that first interview."

She was not encouraging applicants to come in looking like they had just won the "Best Dressed" award at the senior prom. She was talking about the level of regular daily attire, for where she worked, or perhaps a smidgen above.

> *Always make sure your fly's done up, whatever you're wearing.*
>> Pierce Brosnan, actor, named "most stylish man" by *US* Magazine

Knowing what to wear on the day of your interview is vitally important. Some information can be found in books and articles and some can be had by asking friends and acquaintances. But the best way of all to learn about appropriate attire is to go to the workplace and observe what the employees are wearing. Watch people coming into the building in the morning or out at night. If there are elevators, ride them, up and down, two or three times. If there is a company cafeteria, go have a cup of tea and see if you can identify people who are doing the kind of work you want to do, just by the way they dress.

Restaurants in the area will give you an idea of what's considered proper dress. So will professional meetings, service club lunches, and trade shows. Pay more attention to the professionals in the booths at these shows than to the browsers in the aisles.

HOW TO DRESS

You don't need a lot of clothes to dress well for an interview, but what you have should be of good quality, properly fitted, clean, and well pressed. Here are some other ideas on how to dress:

> *The way you dress and the look of your office tell the candidate about your self-image and how seriously you are taking the interview.*
>
> Martin John Yate, *Hiring the Best*

▲ While you want to dress a little above the day-to-day level for the work environment, you do not want to appear so elite that you will have trouble relating to your prospective coworkers.

▲ Pick clothes that you feel good in, made of fabrics you like, in colors that are flattering; be sure you are comfortable in your clothes, both physically and emotionally.

▲ Wear your clothes, don't let your clothes wear you.

▲ Dress in character, not in costume. Make your clothes part of a consistent message about your identity.

▲ If you want to spark up your appearance, accent your basic outfit with a new shirt or blouse or shoes or pocket square.

▲ Wear the college tie or scarf of your school where that is likely to be a plus for you.

▲ The Ivy League look is perfect where the people you will be seeing, and who will be interviewing you, are also Ivy League types. In other situations, the Ivy League look could send out signals of elitism and snobbery. Try to find out the "social" or "class" aspects and attitudes of the company you are interviewing with. Sometimes, though, it will happen that a non-Ivy company will want an Ivy League type because they think it will add "class" to their public image. Don't assume, investigate.

▲ Go in a jogging suit if you are applying for a job as an aerobics instructor. But make sure the suit fits well, is in a color that's flattering to you, and that it is clean and fresh-smelling.

▲ Check out your clothes well in advance in case there should be a stain, missing button or small tear.

▲ Don't let too much perfume or aftershave overwhelm the most attractive scent of all—your natural, fresh smell after a bath or shower.

▲ Be sure to give yourself five minutes of check-up time in front of a mirror to make sure your hair is neat and your tie or scarf is knotted properly.

Dress as though you have already won the job and done it well enough to be able to afford the clothes that achievement would bring. Like the salesman in the $600 suit, look like you have already achieved the success you aspire to.

> If you can accomplish nothing else, presenting yourself as a person who is capable of the job he wants, or has been given, is an acceptable goal.
>
> John T. Molloy, *Molloy's New Dress for Success*

You could also take a course in how to dress effectively, like the one-day dressing seminar I did with Robert Panté. Panté is an author and internationally known authority on dressing, and I learned a lot in his workshop, particularly how important simplicity, elegance, and orderliness are in creating a winning impression.

How about you? What do you need to do to be dressed right for your next interview?

HOW NOT TO DRESS

Always think about the impression you want to make and what clothes will create that impression. Remember that there are also ways *not* to dress for an interview, for example:

> When I tell conservatively dressed businessmen that most men dress for failure, they generally agree.
>
> John T. Molloy, *Molloy's New Dress for Success*

▲ *Suggestively:* If people look twice at you it should not be because of a plunging neckline or an open shirt showcasing chest hair.

▲ *Uncomfortably:* Avoid the wrap skirt that doesn't stay closed when you sit down or the pants that are too tight.

▲ *Without rehearsal:* Make sure that you have worn this outfit before and know how to be a star in it.

▲ *Unorthodoxly:* Unless you are applying for a job as creative director at an advertising agency.

▲ *For another climate:* You do not want to be drenched in perspiration or covered with goose bumps halfway through your interview.

▲ *Like you don't care:* Everyone wants to feel that you care enough about them and their organization to dress well. It is a sign of self-respect and respect for others to dress attractively and appropriately.

▲ *Formally:* Do not come far more formally attired than those around you, making them feel inferior and you look foolish.

▲ Unpressed, unpolished, unclean.

> *Wear your most smashing outfit:*
> *maybe something a bit kooky*
> *that you'll have to live up to.*
> Barbara Walters

Barbara Walters' words are from her book *How to Talk With Practically Anybody About Practically Anything* and are actually advice to the woman about to go out in the world on a day when she doesn't feel so wonderful. In that context, it is probably good advice. It is also good advice in interview situations where the job requires flair, pizzazz, and creativity. The real reason for including it, however, is that in dressing for interviews, as in life, rules are made to be broken. In interviewing too, as in life, it is essential to know the rules and then be innovative, true to yourself, and the very best that you can be.

FREE AT LAST

Did you see yesterday's headline? THE WORKING WOMAN'S POWER SUIT IS HISTORY! After twenty years of formula dressing, the article says, there's new sartorial freedom for women in the workplace. Today the parameters are set by good taste: not attracting undue attention to, or distracting from, what you are saying or doing. That means avoiding wild prints, flashy colors, overly bold accessories, and extreme styles. Choices about hemlines, dresses versus suits, skirts versus pants, styles, and colors can now be based on what is most flattering to your own body shape, personal style, facial features, and coloring. If in doubt, consult an image consultant or work with a professional shopper; both are members of a new industry emerging in response to the needs of working women . . . and men.

> *It is imperative that we dress well if we want to experience life at the top.*
>
> Robert Panté, *Dressing to Win*

CHAPTER TWELVE

MIND POWER

THE human mind is a wonderful servant, but a horrible master. When we enlist the power of our minds to help us achieve our aims in life, we have the best possible resource: guru, genie, and computer wizard, all at our service instantly. But if we allow our minds to dominate us, to make us fearful and insecure, we have subjected ourselves to tyranny of the worst possible kind.

When John F. Kennedy spoke before the 1960 Democratic National Convention he used his wonderful mind to prepare for the event and to manage all the activities leading to that momentous address. But that same wonderful mind drove Kennedy to a self-destructive nervousness that eventually drew blood. Because, at that point, Kennedy's mind was less servant than master.

> *Inner confidence is the key to making genuine contact with another person. Nervous people are too involved with their own alarm bells and flashing signals.*
>
> Barbara Walters

THREE MIND GAMES

How do we use our minds to help us in interviews and in the other momentous events of our life? Here are three ancient and proven approaches, each powerful, each with a lighter side.

Affirmations   come first. These statements of belief assert what we know to be true . . . despite what demonic voices might deny. Affirmations are positive statements about ourselves that we repeat over and over in our heads, ten, twenty, a hundred times. They always start in the first person singular, they always include our first name, and they always include at least one fact about ourselves. For example:

"I, John, am a skillful writer."
"I, Suzie, am an excellent trainer."
"I, Bill, am an outstanding computer programmer."

These come from our self-knowledge and they reinforce what we know to be true. They support the activity ahead of us, whether it is a job interview or a public address. They are not a substitute for hard work and are most effective when we have adequately prepared for whatever is coming next in our lives.

What happens when you start a new affirmation is that the mind responds, "No way! That's ridiculous!" Then, "Well, maybe." And finally, "Yes, that sounds right." What also happens is that when your mind is occupied with affirmations, it cannot be whispering, "You are going to stumble or fall or forget what to say." When you are doing affirmations, your mind is your servant, not your master.

Visualizations come next. In this mind game, we run images through our heads of future events. It is as though we have videotaped a speech or an interview and we are playing it, rewinding, and playing it again. If we don't know the exact setting, we create it. If we don't know what another person in the video looks like, we imagine it. If we don't know exactly what we will be wearing when the event actually happens, we guess.

See yourself walking into an office for the perfect job interview. See the person across the desk smile at you. Watch yourself answering questions with confidence and poise. Notice how the other person nods. Watch how you handle the challenging moments of the interview. Then hear the magic words, "When can you start?" and notice how you feel.

COACHING TIPS

Try the power of affirmations on some simple activity you will be doing later today, like preparing a meal or meeting a friend. Now visualize yourself in the same activity. Notice how this makes you feel as you do it; notice how the activity turns out.

Once when I described this exercise in a workshop, a man in the room said, "I know all about that." Five years earlier he had gone to Dallas for a job interview and stood before the mirror in his hotel room and imagined himself getting the job offer and saying, "Why, yes, I would be delighted to join your company." As he told the workshop, the real event was just the way he visualized it . . . except that the pay was twice what he expected.

If visualizations worked for this man, for the Swiss Olympic bob-sledding championship team, and for other successful people around the world, they will work for you.

It's OK to imagine yourself being successful. Remember the words of Buckminster Fuller, the visionary inventor of the geodesic dome:

> . . . *You do not belong to you. You belong to the universe. The significance of you will remain forever obscure to you, but you may assume you are fulfilling your significance if you apply yourself to converting all your experience to the highest advantage of others.*

Visualize yourself having the best success you can imagine. When it comes true, you will have done something wonderful for yourself, and also for all those you serve. Do this as you drive to your next interview. Do this when you start to wonder What if I blow it? What if I get asked about my last boss? What if they discover that I'm just an ordinary person? Your mind is a servant that never tires. Let it serve you well.

> *There was something about her—a calmness, a radiance—that made me sure she was right for the job.*
>
> Vice President, Human Resources

Centering is the third way to use your mind in preparing for the important moments in life. Centering gets you reconnected with the core wisdom of your being, the calm place within, the essence of who you are. You can center yourself at any time, but a particularly good time is in the two or three minutes before you walk in for a job interview.

Several years ago, a young man came to my office looking for ideas on how to be successful in a job interview scheduled for eleven the next morning. He seemed nervous, so I asked how he intended to settle himself down before the interview. "Two or three beers should do the trick," he replied. Which is when I told him about centering, as a much better way, and gave him these instructions.

Start by taking three deep breaths. Feel the tension pour out of your body each time you exhale. Let go of the frustration and fear and anxiety you have been carrying. Straighten your posture and notice how your energy picks up.

Close your eyes if you can do so safely and comfortably. Visualize a point in the center of your body just behind your navel. See that point as an expanding sphere of white light, clearing away the negativity and nervousness, and making room for the affirmations and visualizations you did earlier.

Like visualization, centering is a mind game used by athletes, astronauts, and peak performers of all kinds. You have the same access to such power for releasing your potential as they do.

A young woman in one of my career-change workshops was working in human resources at the Monsanto Company in St. Louis. On some days, she told us, the CEO of Monsanto, John Hanley, would give her a ride to work in his limo. They didn't speak with each other because that was the time Hanley, a widely respected executive, used for his daily meditation. "If that stuff worked for Mr. Hanley," she concluded, "then who am I to doubt it?" And so, for this young woman, centering became a part of her own successful life.

UNEXPECTED HELP

When you play the three mind games described in this chapter, you signify commitment to your goal. You step over the line from "Wouldn't this be nice," to "Yes, this is what I want." The result is unexpected help, the appearance of allies and assistance where you never would have expected them.

When you fill your mind with the words and images of the result you seek, you prepare yourself for success in ways you can not anticipate. You will be happily surprised by unexpected phone calls, flashes of insight, and encounters with long-lost friends. In spite of your careful planning, new opportunities will come your way and lead to outcomes you never dreamed of.

If you bring more commitment to your job search—and I promise you this is true—the results will delight you.

THREE

Getting Results

▲

CHAPTER THIRTEEN

THE PYRAMID PROCESS

W HEN Paul Hartzell, baseball pitcher turned sales executive, was offered his current job, his new boss was five hundred miles away on a car phone. Over the hum of road noise, Paul heard about the responsibilities, the perks, and the pay. It was not your traditional interview.

For the job before that, the entire interview took place in Mulhern's Tavern. The questions, the decision, and the offer all happened over a long lunch. Again, a nontraditional format.

In both cases, however, Hartzell touched all the bases on his way to the job offer. In baseball as in interviewing, it is important to know how the game works. In interviewing, however, the image that works best is not the diamond but the pyramid.

Why is an interview like a pyramid?

One of the most ancient shapes created by humankind, the pyramid dates back at least 4600 years to the banks of the river Nile. Like those historic monuments, the job interview must be skillfully built, one piece at a time.

Consider the base.

For a pyramid weighing hundreds of tons to last thousands of years, the base had to be solid. For an interview to have a lasting impact, it too must have a solid base.

Interviews must be built on solid information and solid preparation. The information must be the best possible self-knowledge, company knowledge, and industry knowledge. The preparation should include practice interviews, preliminary interviews, and mental rehearsal. A lot must happen for an interview to be successful before two people even set eyes on each other.

THE OPENING RAP

And when those eyes do meet for the first time, the most immediate challenge is to establish a harmonious relationship, an affinity with each other, a rapport. The relationship established at the outset is the foundation on which the entire interview will be built. Unless it is good and solid, all that follows may come tumbling down.

> Establish rapport. Greet the interviewer with a welcoming smile, immediate eye contact, and high energy.
> Tom Jackson, *Guerrilla Tactics in the Job Market*

An important piece of the relationship is agreeing on what is going to be covered. Successful interviewers take a moment at the beginning to set the agenda, however briefly and unobtrusively, except in the rare case where the agenda is absolutely clear to both participants without being mentioned.

Sometimes it is valuable to agree on how the interview will develop as well as what will be covered. So sometimes, in addition to the agenda, skillful interviewers review procedures: what will happen, how long it is scheduled to take, who else might be involved.

One way to remember these three steps in building the base for a successful interview is to think of the word "rap," slang that came into use in the sixties to describe a friendly, informal conversation among friends. Rapport, Agenda, and Procedure are all covered in the initial RAP.

THE PERSON GAP

The great bulk of the interview, once the base is laid, is filling in the space as you move upward, closing the gap as you build toward the apex. In ancient Egypt this was done with stone. In an interview, it is done with dialogue, information, and agreements.

> *Each of you has questions in the interview—both you and the employer. The essence of the interview is that each of you is trying to find out the answers to those questions.*
> Richard N. Bolles

The first gap to fill, the one at the very beginning of the interview, is the interpersonal gap. On both sides there is an unknown area, a vacuum asking to be filled. This is where the critical human questions are considered: How is the chemistry? How is the fit? How will this person, with these skills and interests, match the human requirements of the job?

This person gap—let's call it the P Gap—requires asking and answering questions on both sides. This part of the interview works best where there is good self-knowledge and good preparation on both sides. This part works best if there is a healthy level of candor and self-disclosure.

THE ORGANIZATION GAP

Somewhere in this phase of the interview, the focus shifts from interpersonal issues to organizational issues. This usually occurs when both sides have developed enough trust and confidence in the outcome to want to consider the core issue of any interview: How could we make this a better company? How well could we solve the problems integral to this job?

> *I ask senior managers: Can you define the mission of this company? Is it knocking off competitors or benefiting all mankind?*
> Tom Day

Filling this organizational gap, the O Gap, requires the ability to draw out information not just about the job but also about the problems inherent in the job. In filling the O Gap, the successful candidate uses focus, tact, and active listening. The tone set by both parties should be one of genuine concern for learning about the situation and a willingness to be honest about how good the match is between applicant and organization. Questions should be answered with clarity and candor.

These are the crucial organizational questions: What are the most important challenges I would be facing for the organization? How well do my skills, knowledge, and passions match those challenges? What else might be involved, on either side?

If this inquiry is marked by cooperation on both sides of the desk, and a shared commitment to finding the right answers, the interview moves toward a natural conclusion.

CLOSURE

The peak of the pyramid, its apex, is where the monument stops and the sky begins. In much the same way, the conclusion of an interview is where it all comes together and the future begins. The base has been laid and the gaps filled. Now it is time for completion.

Completion comes from agreement. In a job interview, where many issues have been opened up, this is called closure. Closure comes when we ask, "How does this all sound to you?" Even better, it can come when we hear, "When can you start?"

> *Good employers realize that there is PR value to be gained from everyone who walks through the door. They do not give people reasons to be vindictive.*
>
> Tom Day

Once closing agreement has been reached—whether in the form of a job offer, a decision to go a step further, or a rejection—it is important to express appreciation. "Thank you for what you told me about the company" not only expresses an important sentiment, it encourages future openness.

If all is not clear, return to procedures: Where do we go from here? When will it happen? Who will be involved? If a confirming letter needs to be written, perhaps describing a job offer, this is the time to clarify that. Everyone should know what comes next.

Make sure, always, that you send a follow-up letter, even if it has only been an exploratory interview. Here is how your letter might look:

> *Your home address*
> *City, state, & zip*
> *Your phone number*
> *Today's date*

Ms./Mr. Full name, title
Correct company name
Correct address

Dear Ms./Mr. _____:

Thank you for taking the time to meet with me this morning. Thank you, too, for valuable insights on the computer software industry.

My conversation with you reinforces my determination to pursue a career in computer programming. As you suggested, I will contact Steve Smith at Advanced Software Systems.

I will stay in touch, as you asked and hope that you will do the same.

> *Sincerely,*

> *Your full name*

Write such a letter after *every* face-to-face interview, because you are a polite person, of course, but also because it offers you another exposure to someone who might be able to help you. It puts your name and address on the desk of a person who might want to give that information to the prospective employer who calls or stops by the next day. Think of the thank-you note as an integral part of any interview.

One way to remember these three last pieces of the interview is to think of the capstone on the pyramid. Closure, Appreciation, and Procedure come together to create the CAP.

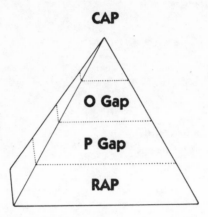

Now how do you put all these essential steps in interviewing into action? The way to begin is with a winning first impression.

▲

CHAPTER FOURTEEN

WINNING FIRST IMPRESSIONS

Sean Connery walks with "the threatening grace of a panther on the prowl," according to one observer, who thinks this contributes to the actor's success in movies and on the stage. Connery credits his distinctive walk to a course he took in body language years ago in London. His teacher was a ballet dancer, Yat Malgrem.

Whatever the reason, Connery impresses people before he even says a word. Which is important, because no one ever gets a second chance to make a first impression. We may become known, like Connery, and create later impressions that improve on the original perception. But there is only one first opportunity.

What can you do to make the first impression you want? Plenty, both before the interview and as you walk in.

> *They say a dog tests you by coming at you, fangs bared, head and tail up, and if you continue to show no fear, he will back off.*
>
> **Roger Ailes, Campaign advisor to George Bush**

BEFORE YOU WALK IN

Roger Ailes, the political consultant, believes that every human contact is an instant size-up in which a person has about seven seconds to "absorb" the situation. Acting on this principle enabled Ailes to help elect George Bush and it can help you. Whether you're talking to millions or to a manager with the power to hire you, a lot of what happens can be controlled even before the first contact.

There are two ways you can make a difference before you walk in the door: in your preparation and in your presentation.

▲ *Preparation.* This includes your preinterview research on the company, the industry, and the people you will be seeing. It includes the exploratory, informational, and practice interviews you have done. And it includes what you have done with your mind: affirmations, visualizations, and centering.

▲ *Presentation.* This includes clothes that are appropriate, comfortable, and confidence-enhancing. Your attire should fit you and the situation. It should tell who you are and how you feel about yourself. And it should be checked out in the mirror just before going in for the interview. You can also ask someone in the elevator or reception area, "How do I look?" Most people are glad to give you a reaction, and almost always what you hear will make you feel better.

COACHING TIP

If you drive to an interview make sure your car is clean, inside and out. Some employers will go out to the parking lot to take a look—and you might end up driving if the interview includes lunch.

There are other ways you can be sure everything is right before you walk in. You can hire an image consultant (look in the Yellow Pages for listings) who can help you select the right clothes, the right hairstyle, and the right look. You can also spend time with a friend who has a video camera, using it to refine how you look, what you say, and how you act. Your smile, your posture, your gestures, all make a difference in those first seconds.

> *The way you dress is the single most important nonverbal communication you make about yourself.*
>
> Tom Jackson, *Guerrilla Tactics in the Job Market*

AS YOU WALK IN

As you are walking in to the interview there are three things you can do to make the first impression you want. Your presence, your eye contact, and your preverbal behavior all make a difference.

▲ *Presence.* Think how good it feels when you are going to see a friend and arrive with a gift. You can have that same good feeling walking into an interview, but you do not need a package in your hand; your present is your presence. All your attention, your thoughts, your energy—everything!—should be focused on that moment. The way to be fully present is to let go of your frustration, your fear, and your nervousness. Relax. Release your inner light. Let your face shine. Think of yourself as a star, carry yourself like one, and you will become a star!

> *He whose face gives no light,*
> *shall never become a star.*
> William Blake

▲ *Eye contact.* People love to look at stars. Best of all, they love to look at stars who look back. Make your initial eye contact positive, warm, and friendly. Imagine that you are greeting someone you heard good things about and have wanted to meet for a long time. Let your eyes reflect that anticipation. People respond to eyes that are alert, alive, positive, and friendly.

▲ *Preverbal behavior.* If a voice in your head is saying "great to be meeting someone I've heard good things about and have wanted to meet for a long time," then your body will be saying the same thing. You will be active, alive, and responsive. Social scientists say that one reason for John Kennedy's compelling charisma was his posture and the way he moved—the vigor of his stride and the thrust of his jaw. You too can bring an aura of charisma into the room, just by your posture and the way you move.

The main event of the first impression is often the handshake, a crucial moment for conveying positive energy. There are many ways to shake hands, and *Working Woman* magazine has identified five of them:

▲ "The Limp Fish," a weak grasp signaling timidity.

▲ "The Karate Chop," a jarring clasp that intimidates.

▲ "The Three-fingered Claw," where two or three fingers are thrust out, signaling that the gesture is merely obligatory.

▲ "The Interview Shake," a solid but not steely grasp and brisk shaking that communicates "glad to meet you." This is the one that makes for a winning first impression.

▲ "The Seal-a-Deal Shake," firm, warm, and accompanied by eye contact that says "trust me, you made the right decision in offering me this job." Save this for leaving a lasting impression at the end of the interview.

In a graduate sales management course I once led, I had an IBM personnel executive come in to talk with the class about interviewing. As an experiment, I asked for a volunteer from the class to do a mock interview with this man, whom no one had ever seen before. As part of my instructions, I told the class that the hypothetical job would be in large computer sales, a position with which our IBM guest was familiar. I set up two chairs in front of the class and then brought in the IBMer and introduced him to the class volunteer, an articulate, assertive man of twenty-five.

As they settled themselves and exchanged pleasantries, I followed the sweep second hand on my watch and at ninety seconds I called, "Stop!"

Then I asked the class: "What were your first impressions of these two people?" Half a dozen or so of the thirty in the room spoke up and most of these were impressed with the man from IBM. Several, however, expressed reservations about their classmate.

Next I asked the volunteer how he felt. "Uncomfortable," he told us. "I figured I could snow this guy, and it didn't seem to be working."

Then the IBM executive spoke. "I felt fine," he told us. "I do a lot of interviewing and I do it well. But I did not have a good first impression of this candidate, who seemed pushy and manipulative."

An interview is not a snow job. Deceit and manipulation in interviews sooner or later lead to problems for everyone involved. You never ever want to try to be something you are not. You always, however, want to be everything that you can be.

In fairness to the student volunteer, he had only a few moments to prepare for his interview with IBM. Another time, he told the class, he would come in properly prepared and with a less aggressive, more cooperative attitude.

In that classroom simulation, we checked first impressions after a minute and a half. We could have cut it shorter or we could have gone longer. One expert says that 50 percent of the decision is made in the first thirty to sixty seconds.

However much time it takes, everyone agrees that first impressions have a huge impact on interviewing success. Those initial visual images, sensations, and feelings when two people first see one another are all important.

> *The most consistently endearing human trait is warmth.* Everyone responds to the person who radiates friendliness from a serene core.
>
> Barbara Walters

When you walk into an interview, operate from a serene core. Be friendly. And, like Sean Connery, walk with grace and confidence.

CHAPTER FIFTEEN

THE OPENING RAP

WONDERFUL as it is in many ways, the Harvard Business School has a tendency to breed arrogance in some of its students. Especially those like me. So in the spring of my second year, when I started scheduling job interviews, I thought, "I sure know a lot about interviewing. After all, I got a super job last summer in San Francisco, the city of my choice, and here I am about to graduate from the best business school in the world. I sure know a lot!"

My first interview was with General Foods, and the placement center gave me a time, a room number, and the name of the man I was to see: Victor Bonomo. I had my Harvard suit, my Harvard résumé, and my Harvard arrogance. What I didn't have was the right building, and by the time I realized my mistake and raced down the street, I was ten minutes late for a thirty-minute interview.

Goodbye, General Foods.

> *Run your life on Lombardi time:*
> *Always arrive ten minutes early.*
> *Winners keep Lombardi time.*
>
> Vince Lombardi, football
> coach

I knew the minute I dashed into the room and gave my sad story to an unsmiling Vic Bonomo that all was lost. Having learned where the interviews were held, I was more successful with Procter & Gamble and ended up working in Cincinnati. Bonomo went on to senior positions at GF and was later president of Bon Ami, but alas, we never met again.

I realize now that what happens in the first minute of an interview is critical. Besides being on time—and ten minutes early is better—it is essential to build rapport in those first moments.

RAPPORT BUILDING

Rapport is a French word, in both origin and pronunciation. It comes from the Old French *raporter,* meaning "to bring back," and from the Latin *portare,* meaning "to carry." The implication is that good rapport will carry a relationship. Sometimes rapport can reconnect a relationship that was already there and needs only to be re-established, and sometimes good rapport can quickly bond a new relationship.

Rapport starts to build with the very first eye contact, before even a word is spoken. It grows from the first verbal exchanges and continues throughout the interview, and sometimes well beyond that.

> First and foremost, make the candidate comfortable and relaxed as early and as quickly as you possibly can.
> Martin John Yate

Inexperienced interviewers often rush past this critical stage without allowing time—a few seconds or, more rarely, a few minutes—for establishing the human connection. Here are four practical approaches to building initial rapport:

▲ *Pleasantries.* Probably the safest initial topics are the weather, the traffic, or the parking—something neutral that gets you both started talking on a simple, nonthreatening level. Though the topic may be mundane, it is OK to be positive. As William Blake says, "Exuberance is beauty."

▲ *Shared experiences.* See a golf photo on the credenza? If you're a golfer, you might ask about it. See a Toastmasters plaque on the wall? If you belong, mention it. Once I was interviewing an Episcopal bishop and the Dag Hammarskjöld words on peace behind his desk gave us a point of common interest from which to start.

> Interviewer: Does flattery work?
> Barbara Walters: A sincere compliment always works.

▲ *Compliments.* A sincere compliment *sometimes* works if it is taste-
ful, relevant, and appropriate. "What a handsome office!" is fine.
"What a nice-looking suit," isn't. Positive reinforcements can be
important anywhere in the interview, to register a point or shift
emphasis. Comments like "I really agree with that" or "Your idea
makes a lot of sense" are good rapport builders.

▲ *Gratitude.* Sometimes it works to show that you respect the
value of someone's time by expressing thanks right in the beginning. I like to do this, but I am careful not to imply that my time
isn't valuable too. The aim is to build a cooperative, participative
relationship in the interview. Showing respect at the outset can
further this aim.

Some people are easy to build rapport with, and some are hard.
Be prepared for either by thinking in advance what you might say.
What do you know about the person? Their background? Their style?
Imagine that you are in their chair and think about what you would
like to hear from someone coming in for an interview.

AGENDA SETTING

How do you know when rapport building has gone on long
enough? One way is to check on the territory you are about to cover,
with agenda-setting questions like these:

"As we discussed on the phone, I am interested in learning about
the public relations function here, the work you do, and the
people who do it. Is there anything else we should plan to cover?"

"As I understand it, we will be talking about the assistant con-
troller's position and how I might fit in. Is that correct?"

"Mr. Jones tells me that I would work closely with your department in the regional sales manager position I am interviewing
for, and he suggested that we get to know one another. Is that
your understanding of what we want to cover in the next few
minutes?"

> *Setting the agenda is a valuable control technique. Most people just sit down and wait for the interviewer to pick up the ball and run with it. The instant they walk in the room, they surrender control.*
> Tom Day

The moments spent on setting an agenda are valuable *any time* people sit down together to achieve some purpose. Practice this skill at meetings and business lunches, starting today, and impress your associates with how clear and focused you are. The more significant benefit is that you will be prepared to use this skill in your next interview, demonstrating the kind of interpersonal expertise that just about everyone wants in those they hire.

PROCEDURES

The agenda is the *what* of an interview, the content. Sometimes it is also valuable to establish the *how* of the interview, the process. Procedure in an interview includes time, people, and activities. Check it out, because if you aren't aware of the procedure, you may be in trouble if . . .

. . . you assume that you have an hour-long interview and the person across the desk is thinking twenty minutes.
. . . you think it will be all conversation and the interviewer plans on having you take a written test.
. . . you think it will be one-on-one and you find you're to be taken before a four-person committee in five minutes.

> *Openness and candor send powerful—and positive—signals about you and your company's environment.*
> Lee Schweichler

Once you have established rapport, set the agenda, and checked procedures in an initial RAP, you are ready to move into the body of the interview. You may return at various times to renewing rapport or reviewing the agenda or procedures as the interview progresses.

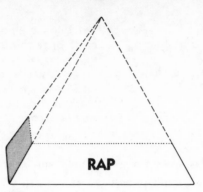

RAP

But you will be building on an established base of understanding and agreement, a strong foundation for all that follows.

In May of 1980, I scheduled an interview with Caspar Weinberger, then a vice president of Bechtel Corporation. In a note confirming the interview time, I said that I was "interested in philosophical views of top executives, like yourself, in connection with my Ph.D. dissertation" and mentioned again how I was "still grateful for your fine speech" two years earlier before a public service group of which I was president. When I arrived at Bechtel and was ushered in for what was scheduled to be a forty-five-minute interview, Weinberger told me that he was leaving for the Middle East imminently and was under great time pressure.

Thus forewarned, I got the most from what turned out to be a seventeen-minute interview. I learned that Weinberger was basically an optimist (because "you are constitutionally required to be this way in California") and a great admirer of "Governor" Reagan, and a lot more.

Whatever the setting, it is important to take the time at the beginning of the interview to establish rapport with the person across the desk, and to check on the agenda and procedures. An experienced interviewer will be doing the same thing and will recognize and respect your skill. An inexperienced interviewer will appreciate your help. Either way, the right start goes a long way toward creating the right result for both players.

▲

CHAPTER SIXTEEN

PERSON TO PERSON

MAX DePree is chairman of the Herman Miller Company, a successful furniture manufacturing company founded by DePree's father. In a little book called *Leadership Is an Art,* DePree describes some of the ideas that have made his company a leader in exemplary management.

"Shared ideals, shared ideas, shared respect, a sense of integrity, a sense of advocacy, a sense of caring," he writes, "are the basis of Herman Miller's covenant and value system." DePree believes that employees should be owners because "people need to be liberated, to be involved, to be accountable."

Employees may own stock or, by virtue of their commitment, they may "own" the challenges, purposes, and goals of an organization. Either way, they are involved. Companies seeking involved employees look hard for indicators in job interviews. Those who want to fully commit themselves in the work part of their lives look for the same kind of indicators from management.

> *We look for team players here—*
> *people who can become stars*
> *by working well with others.*
>
> President, computer software
> company

PERSONAL ISSUES

Personal issues predominate in the early part of an interview, whatever the stated agenda. This assessment process begins with first impressions and initial interchanges and continues into some of the most crucial areas of the interview. The nature of the personal component depends on the nature of the interview: If it is an exploratory interview, the face-to-face chemistry is less important than the information gleaned about prospective work environments and what the fit might be like. If it is a commitment interview, on the other hand, the quality of the interaction with the person across from you is critical. How does this person and his or her organization fit with your impression of what is best for you? How do you fit with their impression of what is best for them?

The issues are illustrated in interlocking circles:

Exploratory   **Commitment**

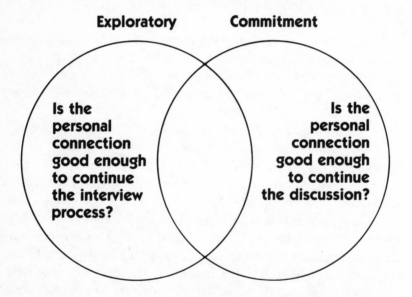

The more-interesting people have often had twists and turns in the road of their personal lives. We look for interesting people.

Admissions Director, Stanford Business School

TELL ME ABOUT YOURSELF

Whatever kind of interview it is, interested employers want to know what you are like. This is expressed in many ways, but what the words are really saying is, "Tell me about yourself."

Asked without preamble and followed by silence, this request can be devastating. I know from experience. In my early twenties, I was seeking a summer job and had scheduled an interview with the president of a small company. With barely a how do you do? and before my seat had hit the chair he said, "Tell me about yourself."

Into a void of silence, I stumbled and stammered, beet red and sweating. I was not offered the job I sought, but four years later the same man hired me to fill a position in his company that led to the seven best years of my business career. Aside from teaching me the value of patience—good companies always need good people, even if the right job isn't available right now—I learned forever the importance of being prepared for what can be the toughest of all interview questions.

How should I have responded? How should you?

Instead of sitting there stupefied, I would now use that request to summarize my pertinent skills and experiences. Keeping in mind what I had learned beforehand about the company and about the job, I would respond to "Tell me about yourself" with a brief synopsis of how I arrived at this place at this time:

"I am a recent accounting graduate of State committed to working for a Big Eight firm . . ." or

"For the last eight years, I worked in food-service management and now I want to apply that experience in a larger firm . . ."

Or whatever two or three sentences best provide a timely, succinct background statement.

Then I would give the three most important skills I want to employ and illustrate each with a specific example. Although I would never read from my résumé, I would be expressing the key points from that document.

What I would communicate, and what we should all communicate at some point in an interview, is the results of going through the nine steps at the beginning of this book, especially steps 2 and 4, Experience and Gifts.

My response might take three minutes or five or seven. It would be followed by a course-correction question, "Is this what you had in mind?" or "Could I provide more detail on some of this?"

According to one expert, "Tell me about yourself" is the most difficult interview question of all . . . and the one most likely to be asked. "This is where candidates are given enough rope to hang themselves and often do, especially by saying too much." Whether asked or not, you *want* to tell the interviewer about yourself as a person and as a prospective contributor to the organization. You *want* the interviewer to know enough about you to make a favorable decision—even if you have to ask, "May I tell you something about myself?"

If you are prepared, "Tell me about yourself" is a welcome request and a perfect opportunity to build a successful interview.

WHAT INTERVIEWERS REALLY WANT TO KNOW

In the last two or three interview stages, organizations see you as a prospective member. They want to be sure you will fit in and add value to the organization. They want to be sure that you will not be disruptive, a poor investment of their time and money, or cause more problems than you solve. Like the Dean of Admissions at Stanford, they want to know if you've learned from your life or just passed through. So you get questions like these:

"Why are you interested in this job?" (They want to know about your motivation and how much you know about yourself.)

"Why are you interested in joining this organization?" (Again, a motivation question, where good research will give you a solid answer.)

"Tell me about your last/current job?" (They want to know what kind of performer you are and how you fit in there.)

"What do you consider your greatest accomplishment?" (They want to know about your skills and what you value most highly.)

"Where do you want to be five years from now?" (They are looking for values, motivation, and self-image.)

"What do you like most about yourself?" (This is from a Taco Bell executive who uses it often because of the unrehearsed answers she gets.)

There can also be some tough questions at this stage:

"How do you recognize good people at work?" (Think about how you measure excellence, in yourself and others, and you will be ready for this one.)

"Why did you leave/are you leaving your current job?" (Tell the truth, in positive terms, and forget about justifying yourself.)

"If your last boss and I were playing golf and I asked him what you were like, really and truly, what would I hear?" (Be brutally honest with yourself and you will be ready for a question like this.)

> *Rifle-shooting questions, with no theme, leaping from one topic to another, keeps the candidate on guard. The end result is that you never get below the surface.*
>
> Tom Day, Advising Management

"What is your biggest weakness?" (Respond with a strength carried too far: "I work too hard" or "I demand too much of my subordinates" or "I am too tenacious" or "I sometimes get too involved working on customer problems.")

"What is your biggest fear?" (As with the weakness question, make this a positive: "I fear being unprepared and often work late the night before a big meeting" or "I hate missing goals and am sometimes accused of overkill.")

YOUR QUESTIONS

As all this is going on, you are forming your own impressions of the personal side of the equation. Like the interviewer, you want to know how you would fit in. Part of what you can learn comes from the behavior of the interviewer and the questions asked. Part of it comes from questions you might ask, such as these:

"What kind of people typically work out best in this organization?"

"What was the previous person in this job like?" (or if the position is a new one, in comparable jobs).

"What kinds of skills and attitudes do you look for in people you promote?"

"Long term, what does this organization value most in people?"

"How important is teamwork here?" (For more ideas on questions see the Interview Guide on page 160.)

Asking questions like these elicits valuable information, unless you are dealing with an unskilled or hostile interviewer. It also impresses the person across the desk with the intensity of your interest. That you care enough to ask these questions is an important indication of your motivation.

> *Bad hiring decisions are harder than ever to fix. It's like getting married: Act in haste and repent at leisure.*
>
> Vice President, Human Resources

TWO PACKS A DAY

Jane Amsterdam's dilemma was broadcast in a recent newspaper item. Recently fired as editor of the *New York Post*, she was perfect for the job of associate editor of the *Los Angeles Times*, a position which had just been offered to her. There was a hitch, however. The LA office in which Amsterdam would be working has a policy against smoking anywhere in the building, and she goes through two packs of Marlboros daily.

If you're in the habit of smoking two packs a day and the place you want to work is a smoke-free environment, some accommodation will have to be made if there is going to be a fit. Probably the one doing the accommodating will be you.

Drinking, too, can be an issue. In jobs where entertaining is involved, an employer may want to know how you handle alcohol. You may be invited to dinner, and you may be evaluated, in part, by how you respond when orders are taken for cocktails or a glass of wine. If you accept a drink, you will certainly be evaluated by how much you have and how you behave.

COACHING TIP

As Americans consume less and less alcohol it is becoming more acceptable to order mineral water with a slice of lime in just about any social situation. In job interviews, a nonalcoholic beverage is the safest course.

I learned volumes about the role of drinking in a job I once applied for. In an early interview, the vice president of sales, with whom I would be working closely, talked about the importance of socializing in the company. I thought about that for a moment and then asked, "Would it be a problem if I didn't drink?"

"No problem."

"OK."

"Absolutely none at all."

"OK."

"Just because some of our customers or salespeople might feel uncomfortable doesn't mean that you should."

I took the job and a year later I was gone. When I talked with the president about why it hadn't worked out, one of the things he said was, "You made us feel uncomfortable."

Part of connecting on a person-to-person level is learning about smoking, drinking, and other eccentricities of the organizational culture. Make sure you know what's important to you and what's important to them. In your job search, look for a place where you are going to be comfortable, where who you are fits with how they are.

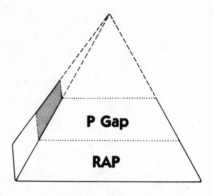

▲

CHAPTER SEVENTEEN

EYE-TO-EYE

"WHAT was the most awful thing that ever happened on your show?" an interviewer once asked Dick Cavett.

"The man who dropped dead during the program," replied Cavett, giving a name. "He was a health expert. No matter how many times I tell it, people laugh, because of the black comedy of the fact that, moments before, he said, 'I'm going to live to be a hundred . . . I never felt better.'"

Sometimes people say one thing and do another. Sometimes words come out of the mouth that the rest of the body refutes. The discrepancy is not usually as dramatic as in the story Cavett tells, and the evidence is usually more subtle. But there are always extra-verbal clues about what is really going on with people for the astute observer to read.

In interviews, where so much is at stake in so little time, it is essential to read *all* the signals, of which words are but one. What it all boils down to is mastering the subtle secrets of communication, the human give-and-take on conscious and often subliminal levels.

Based on the Latin word *communis,* or "common," communication is about creating a common ground on which people can stand side by side. Those who aspire to create such a common ground must learn where other people are standing and what it takes to come stand beside them. Standing together on this common ground is essential if an interview or a job is to work, if life itself is to work.

*Decisions are made emotionally.
The only role of the intellect in
decision making is to keep us
from doing something really
stupid.*

Robert H. Waterman, Jr., to
group of CEOs

This means noticing how the other person communicates and responding in ways that establish a common ground. If communication is to work well, it requires adaptability and selectivity in our use of words and gestures, even in how fast we speak or how loudly. This does not mean giving up our identity or our integrity; it does mean being responsive to others. It means being responsive to emotional signals, as Bob Waterman reminds us, as well as to intellectual input. The process is visceral as well as cerebral.

Sensory signals often come in clusters, blended with other nonverbal signals, and they are usually discernible to the alert participant. Most of these signals call for some kind of action shift, a response that comes naturally if we are well prepared and willing to be flexible.

One of the most important messages is in the way words are used.

CONVERSATION CODES

Behind the spoken word and its dictionary meaning is another level of communication. The language of this communication is subtle—the pace at which we talk, the length of our pauses, and the kinds of words we use. We comprehend much of this extra-verbal language instinctively, but social scientists have now done research to make it recognizable, specific, and learnable.

Dr. Donald Moine, a psychologist who studies persuasive people, has identified two useful dimensions of how people talk, a pacing orientation and a sensing orientation.

Pacing, he says, is crucial in the early stages of an interview. If you find someone who talks *veeeery* slowly, do not try to speed them up but instead slow down to match them. If you encounter someone who talks fast, resist the temptation to talk slowly; instead, speed up and match their pace. Maybe everyone in their family talks fast, and if you don't speak at that rate they will think you are a little slow mentally.

*When you lower your voice,
you're making the person come
to you rather than projecting
out to them. They have to listen
a little bit harder to you.*
    Diane Schleifstein, communi-
    cations expert

When you match another person's pace early in an interview, they think, subconsciously, "Ah, this person is like me . . . I like people like me." Once you are linked with another person at this level (remember rapport!) you can move gradually back to your normal conversational pace and into achieving what you think is important in the interview.

Moine has also studied people of different sensory orientations and observed what kinds of words they like to use. Some people, he has found, respond most strongly to auditory signals: "I hear what you are saying" or "That rings a bell" or "Sounds good to me." Others are visual: "I see what you mean" or "Looks great!" or "She's pretty as a picture." Others, and Ronald Reagan is in this category, see things in physical terms: "That hits home" or "He's really up against the wall" or "On a gut level, that sure grabs me."

It is important to match the person you are talking with if you hope to communicate effectively. Listen to the kind of words you are hearing—auditory, visual, or physical—and use them yourself.

There is a new field of study called conversation analysis that examines the complex rules and regularized practices of how we talk with one another. Two scholars in this field, Deidre Boden and Harvey Molotch, in a paper about who dominates talk and who holds power in a conversation, give the example of the interrogation of people accused of being communists by the U.S. House Committee on Un-American Activities in the 1950s. While many witnesses wanted to express themselves before the committee, they were usually stopped cold by the opening question: "Are you now or have you ever been a member of the Communist Party?"

Rarely will a job interview question be so brutal, but having comeback questions and an understanding of how conversation works can help any of us negotiate difficult psychological terrain if we encounter it.

EYE SIGNALS

Each of us is different in the amount of eye contact with which we are comfortable, and for each of us this varies depending on how we feel. In building rapport in an interview, it is as important to find the right level of eye contact as it is to find the right conversational pacing and word selection. To build trust, match the signals of the person across the table.

Sometimes eye signals are obvious—the difference between smiling eyes and glaring eyes is unmistakable. Sometimes they are less obvious: eyes down and away can reveal self-consciousness, shyness, or guilt. Eyes that flare or pinpoint may be expressing surprise or anger.

Eye signals can even have international implications, as in the famous encounter between Lyndon Johnson and Nikita Khrushchev, when the American President "stared down" the Russian. In fact, cultures differ in the amount of eye contact they are comfortable with. Usually, the shyer the people, the less eye contact there is. Japanese are very discreet with their gaze, but Italians look strangers in the eye as they stroll down the *strada*.

Research done by Boston College neuropsychologist Joe Tecce indicates that eyes reveal emotions in another way: negative feelings like pain and anxiety mean more blinks; pleasant feelings mean fewer. During the 1988 presidential debates, Tecce observed, George Bush's average blink rate of sixty-seven per minute rose to eighty-nine when talking about abortion and dropped to forty-four when praising Dan Quayle.

Dentists and psychotherapists observe the blink rate to know when patients are feeling pain. In a job interview, the blink rate is an important eye signal also. More blinks usually indicate tension—time to be alert!—and fewer mean that things are going well.

Eye movement is another clue. When someone's eyes focus first on your right eye and then on your left they are probably interested in what you are saying. No movement and there's no one home. If you want to see this demonstrated, turn off the sound next time a love scene comes on the TV screen and notice the eye flicks of the one being romanced. Not only do eye flicks give the impression we want but they also, according to research, help us retain more of what we hear.

Eyes also reflect thoughts. "I could tell that most candidates were thinking about what they were going to say next," reported a network executive interviewing dozens of people for a prestigious TV job. "The one we hired was one of the few who totally concentrated on me as I talked." Listen. Focus. Give the person across the desk your full attention, and your eyes will be your ally.

BODY LANGUAGE

The body does not usually give as dramatic signals as in the case of the health expert who dropped dead on the Dick Cavett show. But it does give signals, sometimes obvious, other times subtle, often different from the words being spoken by the person inhabiting that body. And we are more likely to be successful in human interactions if we know something about them and how to interpret them.

> *The sharp interviewer wants access to the candidate so he can watch body language in a setting that is more conversational than confrontational. Both parties can hide behind a desk.*
> Tom Day

Notice how close you sit to the interviewer, especially if you are side by side next to a desk or conference table. Be alert to what distance is right for you, and for the person with whom you are meeting. Don't sit so close that you are intimidating or so far away that you seem aloof and disconnected.

In *How to Read a Person Like a Book,* Gerald Nierenberg and Henry Calero describe many different gestures and what they mean, for example:

▲ Openness gestures include open hands; unbuttoning or removing a suit jacket; sitting with legs uncrossed; and sitting across a table, rather than behind a desk.

▲ Confidence is signaled by a proud, erect, open stance; by hand gestures that do not cover the face or mouth; and by the "steepling" hand gesture of fingertips joined together.

▲ Readiness gestures include hands on hips, like the athlete prepared to enter the contest, with legs apart; also sitting on the edge of the chair, eager for action.

▲ Expectancy is conveyed by rubbing the hands together.

▲ Cooperation can be expressed by touching (although this signal can also mean "Everything is going to be all right"), or when one person moves closer to another.

The negative emotions also have their signals:

▲ Nervousness can be communicated in many ways: an averted gaze, crossed legs, fidgeting, jingling coins, clearing the throat, or giving an air-expelling "Whew!"

▲ Defensiveness is suggested by arms crossed, especially when the fists are clenched, or by crossed legs.

▲ Frustration can be inferred from short breaths (like those of an angry bull), from a hand run through the hair, a rubbing gesture along the back of the neck, from tightly clenched hands, or a hand-wringing gesture.

▲ Boredom is dramatized by drumming fingers on a table, by tapping the feet, and by the foot's steady kicking motion at the end of a crossed leg. Boredom is also revealed by placing the head in the palm of the hand and letting the eyes droop ("Woe is me"). Also by doodling, and by a blank, vacant stare. Boredom across the interviewing table means either no one cares or no one is listening, dangerous on both counts for both interviewer and interviewee.

Charles Darwin observed in his extensive research that some animals, when encountering a potential adversary, lie on their backs, exposing their soft underparts and throats to the other. Even the most ferocious predator, Darwin reported, would not take advantage of this posture of complete trust. When we risk being candid and vulnerable in an interview setting, we have the opportunity to defuse hostility and promote cooperation—providing we are able to read the signals correctly.

Many of these unspoken signals can be learned by reading about them, but the most effective way of improving our interpretation of them is through observation and the experience of daily life. There are opportunities we can make use of at work, at play, at home with friends and family. So keep your eyes open, observe carefully the people in the world about you; be alert to what men and women say with words and what they say with gestures.

▲

CHAPTER EIGHTEEN

ON THE INTERVIEW TRAIL

AMONG other things, Jay Conrad Levinson now writes wonderful books about guerrilla marketing and career management, but at an earlier point in his career he wrote advertising copy as Creative Director for the Leo Burnett advertising agency in Chicago. At Leo Burnett, Levinson was on the "interview trail," which meant that just about everyone who was interviewed by the agency spent some time with him.

Besides being known for his creativity, Levinson was known for the noninterview questions he put to job candidates, questions like:

"What kind of music do you like?"
"What are your favorite musical groups?"
"What current movies do you like best?"
"What TV shows do you watch?"
"Which magazines do you read regularly?"

"I talked to them like a friend at a party," Levinson recalls. "I got wonderful insights into their personalities. I learned whether they were living in today's world or yesterday's world. I learned whether they were workaholics or had authentic outside interests."

Everyone on the interview trail at Leo Burnett did a report on the candidates coming through. "Mine helped a lot to flesh out the person," Levinson recalls. "I was often told that my insights made the decision easier."

While some of Levinson's questions would not meet today's legal guidelines, they are still worth thinking about. It is worth contemplating your response to unorthodox interviewers. It is worth considering what you would do if asked, "What kind of music do you like?" The reality is that if you know the kinds of people you are likely to encounter on the interview trail, and if you have some idea of how to react, your journey will be considerably easier.

> *During my interviews at Cambridge University I had a most unusual experience. It was my final meeting of the day, with a senior fellow at Corpus Christi College, and he spent the entire hour lying flat on his back under his table questioning me about New Orleans jazz and early English porcelain.*
>
> Nicholas Owen, British business executive

Jay Levinson and the Cambridge professor who conducted an interview while lying under a table each had his own unique style. As you travel down the interview trail you will find other styles, usually identifiable within the first two minutes of the interview.

Some of the more common of these are described in the paragraphs that follow, each identified by a catch phrase and defined in the simplest of terms. Remember that these caricatures are, in their own way, all serious interviewers. And in the real world of complex flesh-and-blood people, you may see the characteristics of several types blended in one person. You will deal with them more effectively if you know something about them beforehand.

Personality Plus. This type is cordial, polished, and focuses totally on the interview. Personality Plus smiles a lot and quickly puts you at ease by saying things like, "So glad you could come by" and "Putting it in your own words, could you give me some sense of why you're interviewing here?"

Match the warmth and cordiality of this type, without being insincere. Beware of being so taken in by all the good feelings that you don't cover your interview agenda. Because Personality Plus is often hard to read, be sure to get clear feedback and closure at the conclusion of the interview.

The Toucher. One variation on Personality Plus is The Toucher, one of those tactile types who communicate with two-handed handshakes, hands on arms, hands on shoulders. The Toucher sometimes invades our personal space, coming within inches of our face in greeting or sitting uncomfortably close at a coffee table.

> *The most unusual thing that ever happened to me during a job interview was when a job applicant challenged me to arm wrestle.*
> Business Executive

With The Toucher, be willing to touch in return, perhaps just a bit less than what you are receiving and always following your own instincts for what is appropriate. The Toucher wants to connect, so you should strive with this type to do that on the mental and emotional levels, as well as the physical level. Touching is an important power gesture, so use it with sensitivity to status differences, age differences, and gender differences.

The Pleaser. Another variation on Personality Plus is the pleaser, the kind of person who craves continual positive feedback in order to feel OK. This type will watch you closely to be sure you are satisfied with the interaction and is likely to try something new if there is any sign that you are not. Pleasers often use flattery: "How terrific you look today!" or "That was an amazing job you did!" or "How could you accomplish so much in so short a time?"

Pleasers, and Richard Nixon is one, are highly susceptible to flattery. So, within limits, say nice things to these people. But, as with the other types, be sure to cover the agenda of the interview and reach a clear conclusion.

Smartypants. This type talks fast, using lots of words that are polysyllabic (which is Smartypants language for "big"), and often finishes sentences for others. If male, this type usually wears a bow tie, and if female, large eyeglasses. Smartypants will say things like, "Our analysis was insightful but ambiguous" or "Conceptually, what is your perception of this?" or "Can you tell me what suboptimization levels you operated on during that project?"

When interviewing with a Smartypants, talk as fast as they do, but ask for clarification when you need it, "Could you phrase that another way, please?" Smartypants respects experts (most Americans do), so get to topics you know a lot about and spout a little jargon. You will soon notice that Smartypants types flaunt their intelligence mainly to cover feelings of inferiority. Once you win their trust you will find them easily persuaded.

Gruff and Ready. This type talks tough, in blunt, brief, often guttural phrases. Gruff and Ready often has a rigid, military bearing. Hostility is just below the surface with Gruff and Ready, and can usually be seen as fire in the eyes. "Let's get to the point," is a typical kind of comment. Also, "Talk straight!" or "The bottom line here is, can you cut the mustard?"

In an interview with Gruff and Ready, get to the point and keep your responses crisp. Match the tone of voice and pacing that you are hearing, to the extent you can, and make clear, definitive statements. Also ask short, direct questions. Should you get the job, expect an eventual ally in Gruff and Ready, but do not expect warmth or nurturance.

The Detective. Like Gruff and Ready, The Detective is more interested in facts than in social niceties. As with Lieutenant Columbo on TV, the appearance of The Detective is often misleading. Detectives are introverted, investigative people who ask questions like, "Can you give me the specifics on that?" or "Could you explain this four-month gap in your résumé five years ago?" or "What was the rate of return on the new service you introduced?"

Be prepared with lots of facts for The Detective, in your head or in your briefcase. Be direct. Be clear. But don't be too intimidated, because The Detective, once convinced of your abilities, can be a staunch ally.

The Ego. Ego types talk mostly about one topic: "I created that campaign" or "I saw the need to change before anyone else" or "Most of the key players here come to see me before major decisions are made." Because The Ego is so busy with this agenda, not much listening gets done. The Ego usually dresses well, perhaps even foppishly, and may be seen to strut a little.

Feed The Ego what it craves: recognition, praise, and affirmation. But also be sure that you get answers to your questions and make your points in the time available. Check to be sure you are being heard, with questions like, "Does that make sense to you?" Let *your* ego show too, since that language is understood here, and stress your accomplishments as well as your capacity for doing even more in the future.

The Mouth. A first cousin to The Ego is The Mouth, the interviewer who does not know how to stop talking. Where The Ego talks about him- or herself, The Mouth may talk about the company, spewing forth information that even the founder's mother would find boring. The Mouth usually talks too much out of inexperience or nervousness.

> *The winner in the interview is the one who gets the other person to do 80 percent of the talking.*
> Tom Day

Give The Mouth a chance to run, because there may be some things that need to be said before any genuine interaction can take place. Get The Mouth to focus on the issues of the interview, as covered in the opening RAP, and interrupt if necessary. The Mouth is willing to be persuaded and often welcomes support in making the interview productive.

The Eccentric. An eccentric is someone who "departs from the conventional," and in that sense both Jay Levinson and the Cambridge don beneath the table are eccentrics. When you encounter The Eccentric in an interview, you will have one of two reactions: horror or delight. Be prepared, by knowing about the company, the industry, the kinds of people on the interview trail and your experience will be one of delight.

COACHING TIP

On the interview trail ask, "What should I expect from the person I am seeing next? What is he like?" These are intelligent questions and provide useful information.

There are other types besides these, and perhaps you have encountered one or two. What they all have in common is that they want to get the right person into the job being filled. Your goal is to convince the interviewer that *you* are that right person. Once you have a sense of who you are dealing with, your challenge is to adjust and respond to what is happening before you to present yourself as effectively as possible.

When I was interviewing at the Procter & Gamble Company, I was warned about a guy in the Food Division. "He asks weird questions." Sure enough, ten minutes into our interview he says, without any connection to anything,

"What do you think of Abraham Lincoln?"

That kind of question might come from an eccentric, and certainly weirder questions have been asked in job interviews. It might also come from someone interested in seeing how you perform under pressure, someone under the illusion that artificially created stress can help select good people. Now discredited by enlightened employers, as well as those who advise them, stress interviews are from a bygone era. But you should be alert to stress questions, especially no-win variations like these:

"Are you nervous?"

"Would you lie to protect your boss?"

"How do you feel about an occasional extra-marital fling for those who travel a lot?"

You do not have to answer such questions. Instead of trying, respond with, "Is that question relevant to the job we are discussing?" or "Is that part of the job?" If you are talking with the kind of person whose organization you really want to become part of, they will respect your integrity. They will respect you for speaking up. If they don't even know what integrity is, it is better to discover that now. There is already enough pressure felt, by those on both sides of the desk, without the addition of stress questions.

Challenging questions come up in any interview; the whole process is challenging and that is as it should be. Just be prepared for those challenging questions and those who will ask them. Because the more you know about what to expect on the interview trail, the further you will travel.

▲

CHAPTER NINETEEN

THINK LIKE AN OWNER

Bob Waterman, coauthor of *In Search of Excellence,* tells about a client who used an unorthodox approach to get employees to think like owners. According to Waterman, this organization tried everything, from newsletters to employee handbooks to videos. What finally worked was when they asked managers to put nameplates on their desks reading NOT THEY.

The idea was to discourage the mind-set called "They did it," to stop people thinking that someone else was responsible for what was going on, to get people to see the impossibility of complaining to "they." There was no longer "they" or "them," in the language used at this company, just "we" and "us." People worked together, as teammates with shared responsibilities, and got things done better than ever before.

Why? For one thing, owners persevere. They have a deep emotional interest in ideas, causes, missions, or property and do not let rejection or other barriers stop them. They are relentless in pursuit of their goals.

> Every person in the company carries the dignity and the responsibility of ownership.
> Paul Hawken, *Growing a Business*

Owners share both the responsibility and high self-esteem of participation. They focus on results, not on themselves, talk about *our* challenges, *our* problems, *our* rewards. Whether an owner controls the stock in a corporation or the fate of a small department, he or she values talking to others who also think like owners. Owners like people who are involved and participate fully, starting with job interviews.

The unfortunate reality, however, is that most job interviews are not fully participative. Some interviews are primarily passive, where not much happens; others are conducted by some arcane formula with no real heart or substance or relationship to either party's humanity. Even those interviewers experienced enough to rise above such behaviors often indulge in subtle power games. Seen as a hierarchy, with each form more evolved than the one below it, the four approaches to job interviewing look like this:

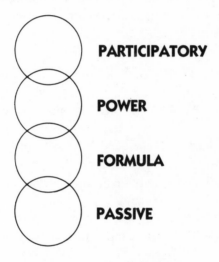

PARTICIPATORY

POWER

FORMULA

PASSIVE

PASSIVE INTERVIEWS

The most rudimentary form of interview is where one or both participants are not actively involved or engaged, where one or both wait for the other to make something happen. Such an "interview" is really a noninterview, a nonevent very unlikely to produce positive results for either side.

In a passive interview, the interviewer might say things like:

"Do you have any particular type of job in mind?"
"I'm not sure why you're here."
"I don't know much about this company."
"It really doesn't matter what we discuss."
"Tell me whatever you feel like telling me."

Obviously this is an interviewer who is not focused on making the interview successful, is not prepared; in fact, doesn't really care. No better is the passive interviewee, who mumbles inanities like:

"I'm not sure why I'm here."
"I don't care if I hear more or not."
"I don't know what excites me most."
"Whenever you want to end is fine with me."

For an interview to work, both sides must have a sense of purpose and commitment to clearly defined, short-term goals. They must be motivated and focused, if necessary using a preset formula for conducting interviews.

FORMULA INTERVIEWS

One level beyond the passive interview, one stage more evolved, is the one structured by some textbook formula. "The less it resembles an interview," Dick Cavett has said, "the better." And I say that the more it resembles an interview, especially one with a particularly rigid structure, the worse it is for everyone.

This book offers a metaphor for an interview, the pyramid, and describes four stages in creating a pyramid-shaped interview. This metaphor is a map that tells where to go but not what will happen along the way. It is intended to illuminate the path, not to be followed slavishly.

Formula is different from process. With a formula, the adherent goes from step to step to some promised, preordained conclusion. With a process like the pyramid process, there is a goal and a vision and unpredictable events along the way. The responsibility for success lies with the people involved, not with the process.

- ▲ Formula is forced, process flows.
- ▲ Formula is rigid, process flexible.
- ▲ Formula is mindless, process challenging.
- ▲ Formula is closed, process open-ended.
- ▲ Formula is deadening, process enlivening.
- ▲ Formula is demeaning, process uplifting.
- ▲ Formula is constricting, process expansive.

When I was a sales trainee at the Procter & Gamble Company, I was taught to sell soap using a formula. Each month sheets would come out listing the benefits of promoted products—a free plastic rose with giant-size Ivory Liquid, say, or ten cents off king-size Tide—and we were encouraged to read these points to the grocer while holding the sales bulletin for him to see. As promised, an order often followed.

You, however, are not a box of soap. Formula selling works for Tide but it will not work, at least not very well, for you.

POWER INTERVIEWS

Power interviews are characterized by one side or the other trying to use some real or imagined advantage to get the result they want. Power interviews can involve manipulation, subtle and not-so-subtle forms of control, and blatant attempts to dominate.

Power has many definitions, and the one that fits best here is "capacity for action." In this sense, both sides have power: the interviewer has the capacity for utilizing and rewarding the efforts of those employed; the interviewee has the capacity for the productive, creative, profit-making activity called work. Besides this, both sides have the power of knowledge about who they are and what they offer. The problem comes when that power is misused.

When power is used to create fear, to intimidate, or to subtly coerce, the final outcome of the interview will not be as positive as it could be. One side or the other will feel misused. Even if there is only a vague sense of this, it is not the best outcome.

> *Elicit information from the applicant before the job is described in detail. If you tell the applicant all about the job and describe the type of person you are looking for, you are providing the applicant with the ideal opportunity to play a role.*
>
> Personnel Manual for a major insurance company

Withholding information is one way to use power, playing a role is another. In an interview, neither side is required to tell everything; such behavior would probably raise questions about the judgment of the person doing the revealing. But neither side should withhold pertinent information. The sequence in which information is released is part of the interviewing game, but all relevant information must be revealed at some point or someone will wind up unhappy.

As an applicant, you should not play a role unless you are able and willing to play the same role every day on the job. Match the communication style of the person across the desk from you in order to connect, but don't be phony. To thine own self be true—and to the interviewer as well.

Other critical power issues are:

Honesty. Always tell the truth: Honesty is not the best policy, it is the only policy. You do not have to tell everything about yourself, but what you do say should be true.

Exaggeration. Avoid this insidious form of dishonesty. Learn instead to become articulate and expressive about your strengths and accomplishments, using authentic data.

Threats. Never make a threat unless you intend to act on it; never make a threat if you want the relationship to thrive and grow.

Games. There is a fine line between being a skillful negotiator in an interview and being a manipulator. Learn where that line is for you and play by the rules.

In power interviews, the urge is for one side to dominate the other, to use whatever advantages can be found to get a desired result. Most interviews today are power interviews, in one way or another, but there is a better way.

PARTICIPATORY INTERVIEWS

The most effective, highest form of interview is one in which both sides participate fully, giving the best they have in open, candid interchange. They share a commitment to the same goal: to make organizations the best that they can be by getting the right people doing the right work. In participatory interviews, both players think like owners.

> *Invite the interviewees to a company softball game, or even a meeting. Make them feel at home. Ask them to criticize the company instead of allowing them to offer up fawning praise.*
>
> Paul Hawken, *Growing a Business*

In a participatory interview the emphasis is on teamwork, not domination. The emphasis is on cooperation, not manipulation. Because so much is at stake, both sides want to pose the right questions and elicit candid answers, and they are willing to give whatever is required to achieve these goals.

Participation is an attitude as well as a behavior. It is a state of readiness, an inclination toward cooperation. The best, most productive attitude to have is to be ready to participate fully in any kind of interview. This is especially vital at the last stages of commitment interviews. You may meet other attitudes and states of readiness, people who operate at the formula or power level, but you should be set to function at the highest level.

To have a participatory interview, both people must be ready and willing to play. For that to happen, you must demonstrate that you are knowledgeable about and seriously interested in the problems you might be given the opportunity to help solve. You must convince the interviewer that participating with you is a good investment of time and energy.

Participation presupposes preparation. If you want to participate fully in an interview, you must know yourself, the company where you would like to work, and the industry in which it operates. Be ready to actively use that knowledge, and be aware that without thorough preparation, there can be no full participation.

In a participatory interview, those involved . . .

. . . agree openly on agenda and procedures.
. . . talk candidly about who they are and what they offer.
. . . make relevant problems clear to one another.
. . . share responsibility for an effective discussion.
. . . arrive together at mutual decisions.

In a participatory interview, you hear things like:

"I want to make this right for both of us."
"How can I be more helpful in answering your question?"
"Is this in line with what you are looking for?"
"I'm willing to adjust to make this more palatable."
"Let's try to resolve this."

Participatory interviewing is the format and process for the future. It is one aspect of the goal of international participation we must strive for if we are to make the world work peacefully and productively.

> *Human evolution is now at a crossroads. Stripped to its essentials, the central human task is to organize society to promote the survival of the species and the development of our unique potentials.*
> Riane Eisler, *The Chalice and the Blade*

A participatory approach to making decisions about work is a concrete step we can take right now to move toward Riane Eisler's dream.

By taking this step, you inspire others to do the same. There is nothing better on the interview trail than encountering a participator, a person willing to share information and power with a prospective new member of the organization, eager to function like a teammate because the organization is seen as a team. Two people coming together to openly explore solutions to problems that concern them both can achieve mutual personal and professional satisfaction.

Zig Zigler, the motivational speaker, puts it this way. "You can get everything you want in this world if you only help enough other people get what they want."

Put his advice into action.

It works.

It can work for *you*.

▲

BE A PROBLEM SOLVER

NOT long ago, I was facilitator for a group of seventy attorneys who came together at a venerable seaside resort to discuss mutual concerns and look for answers to common problems. It was the firm's annual retreat, and between the sumptuous meals and scuba diving expeditions there was some serious talk about how the organization should grow.

On the final day, recruitment was on the agenda: "How can the firm attract and retain the best people?" Everyone present was given a ten-page summary of recruiting statistics, which showed that in the preceding year only about 40 percent of attorneys offered positions with the firm had signed on. A number of issues were raised in the discussion that followed, some with great passion:

"Why don't more candidates accept our offers?"
"How do we sell attractive candidates on joining?"
"How can we get senior partners more involved in recruiting?"
"What can we do about our elitist image?"
"How can we become more effective interviewers?"

Listening to the discussion, I realized that these people had a serious problem: They had a need for good people and were having a hard time filling that need. All of them had once been job hunters, and most of them knew that there are lots of skillful, well-trained people who look for work each year. But that was not their concern.

Those lawyers were concerned about how to get the people

needed to solve their organization's problems and make it function well. They sought people who were eager to accept the challenge of discovering those problems and becoming part of their solution. It is that simple. And that difficult.

> *Your job as owner and manager is not to solve every problem. Your job is to create a company with compelling problems that attract bright, unusual people to join in solving them.*
>
> Paul Hawken, *Growing a Business*

PROBLEM SOLVING

Those with jobs to fill want people to join them in solving problems. They have identified needs and they want to see that these are met, which is what organizations do—they find needs and they fill them. To meet these needs, organizations require capable, motivated people committed to doing their part.

Said another way, a job is an opportunity to solve problems. If an organization can find someone costing $50,000 annually to solve $100,000 worth of problems per year, it is delighted. The job seeker who can talk specifically about his or her problem-solving capacity is using language the organization longs to hear. More valuable still is the job seeker who has learned enough about the problems facing the organization to relate specific skills to their solution: Here is what I can do, based on my proven talent, to solve this particular set of problems you are facing.

How does this work in the interview?

It works best if you have established rapport and agreed on an agenda at the start of the interview. It works best if you have filled the P Gap, have handled your people concerns and those of the person across from you, building trust in the process. Then you can get to the heart of it: the problems facing the organization and the role you might play in meeting them.

This might be called the O Gap, the gulf between the problems of the organization and its capacity to solve those problems. It is the unfilled need that has brought you and the organization together. It is the next stage in building the pyramid of a successful interview.

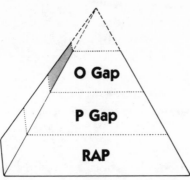

To fill the O Gap, you must first demonstrate an authentic interest in the organization. This starts with your preinterview preparation and continues with your attitude and inquiries early in the interview.

> *On the flight home, I took out a piece of hotel stationery I had saved and began to write a letter, outlining my concepts of what a personal computer should do.*
>
> John Sculley, Returning from his first interview with Apple Computer

When John Sculley drafted his first letter on personal-computer capabilities he was intrigued by Apple—but not at all sure he wanted to work there. "All this was a unique and foreign vocabulary for me," he wrote later. "Yet somehow I knew I could make a contribution." John Sculley demonstrated this willingness to contribute by producing what became an eight-page letter "filled with underlined phrases and words, diagrams, cubes, and boxes of conceptual models and decision-making tools." Contributions early in the interview process paid off for John Sculley and they can pay off for you too.

A word of caution: Be a participator in filling the O Gap, but not a snoop. Don't abuse the goodwill of the interviewer by asking rude or impertinent questions. Make them relevant, as John Sculley did, and listen well.

As you move into this phase of the interview, here are the kinds of questions you might ask:

"Could you tell me more about the responsibilities of this job?" (Responsibilities are problems written as a job description.)

"What are some of the specific challenges the person you hire will be facing?" (A more specific way of asking for the problems involved.)

"How does this job fit into meeting the challenges facing the department/division/company?" (The stated purpose of an organization is lots of little challenges added together.)

"What kinds of things have been successful in the past in meeting these challenges?" (History is an excellent indicator of the future.)

"What kinds of achievements would you most like to see from whomever you hire for this position?" (One way to get challenges translated into objectives. For more ideas on questions, see the Interview Guide on page 160.)

Follow up your questions with "Could you tell me more?" or "Could you give me an example?" or "Could you be more specific?" James Kohlmann, a Florida recruiter, advises, "Ask a steady drumbeat of duty-related questions." Your goal, he says, is "to be a team player who will take the burden from your supervisor's stooped shoulders. You need to ask yourself, 'What's keeping this guy awake at night? How can I help?'"

Between interviews, make notes, perhaps in your "Lessons Learned" journal, so you can build on your knowledge as you go along.

Besides an attitude of inquiry and knowing the kind of questions to ask, it helps to understand the problem-solving process. Problems are solved on the path to the right work, in my experience, much as they are solved in business. It works like this:

▲ *Definition* is the first step in solving any problem. What is really happening? How can it be understood, verbally or in writing, as image or metaphor? The more time spent here, on the job hunt or in the interview, the better the results.

> *Problems are opportunities in work clothes.*
> Henry J. Kaiser

▲ *Options* usually begin to emerge toward the end of the definition stage as the problem becomes clearer. In creating options, don't cut off your imagination too soon: sometimes the last idea is the best one.

▲ *Planning* evolves naturally out of the option stage, as two or three best choices become apparent. What will it take to produce action in the job hunt or with the business problem? What kinds of resources? Applied for how long? With what kinds of benchmarks to measure progress?

▲ *Action* evolves from planning. Sometimes there is a single big step and sometimes there are smaller, sequential steps leading to something big. Action builds on all the previous stages, taking something from each. As action is taken in a job search or in business, there is feedback and the definition of results that link the problem-solving process back to stage one, creating a continuous flow.

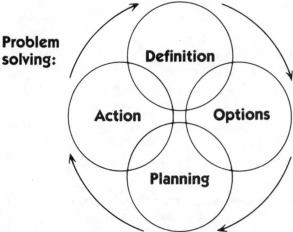

Problem solving:

Definition

Action

Options

Planning

In job interviews, use your knowledge of problem solving to define the challenges inherent in the job for which you are interviewing, to understand what options are available for meeting those challenges, and even to clarify what actions might be called for. Be a skillful asker of questions. Be an active listener.

After hearing about problem-solving power in one of my seminars, the manager of a large retail store was concerned. "There is no way I am going to talk to an applicant about our problems," he insisted. As we talked further, however, it turned out that he appreciated prospective employees who were genuinely interested in the chain and asked intelligent questions. This manager, like many, wants to ask his own questions first but is then willing to engage in real dialogue, especially if an applicant is well prepared and willing to listen. "No one really listens to me," he mused, "and I would be impressed with someone who did."

CREATING PROBLEMS

In a chapter about problem-solving power, it is important to include some words of caution about *problem-creating power*. Organizations want problem solvers, not problem causers. Managers want to add to the company's profits, not its costs. They want people who focus on positive contributions, not negative behaviors. They want people who . . .

    . . . are a force for cooperation, not dissension.
    . . . focus on challenges, not personalities.
    . . . create clarity, not confusion.
    . . . talk about goals, not gripes.
    . . . tell stories, not secrets.
    . . . are reliable, not flaky.
    . . . work hard, as a team member, but not compulsively.
    . . . keep agreements, even when it's hard to do so.
    . . . practice punctuality, even if it means getting up earlier.
    . . . demonstrate loyalty, as a member of the team.
    . . . when they leave the job, make a clean break.

During the interview, be prepared to participate actively in the problem-solving process of the organization, even if it turns out that your talents are not part of the solution. If both sides pursue the truth openly at this stage, they will arrive at an answer that works, ultimately, for everyone.

> *A more effective way for the parties to think of themselves is as partners in a hardheaded, side-by-side search for a fair agreement advantageous to both.*
>
> Roger Fisher and William Ury,
> *Getting to Yes*

If two people focus on their own interests, they become defensive and reactive. If they think collaboratively, solutions come that neither could have expected.

On the path to your next job, think like a partner. Be hardheaded, but aim to cooperate in the search for answers that will be right for everyone involved.

CHAPTER TWENTY-ONE

THE FINE ART OF ANSWERING QUESTIONS

"INTELLIGENT questions," George Keller likes to say, "are the best management tool of all." As chief executive officer of the giant Chevron Corporation, Keller has asked lots of questions.

He still recalls the moment he learned the importance of intelligent questions. "I was working in the engineering department after about eighteen months with the company. I prepared an engineering design proposal for one of our refineries and brought it in to my boss. He asked if I had talked to the refinery general manager, and I said 'I didn't really want to bother him about this, because I thought this was something we could handle.' And my boss said, 'George, there is nothing more flattering than to ask someone an intelligent question.' "

George Keller encourages people to ask the intelligent question, and not just because it's flattering. As he demonstrates in his life and in his work, there is an art to asking such questions, just as there is an art to answering them. Both begin, oddly enough, with learning the fine art of listening.

LISTENING WELL

Listening is not a spectator sport; it requires active participation. This means actively encouraging the person who is doing the talking with your close attention. You can improve your commitment to hearing what is being said by practicing these four steps for active listening:

> *I interviewed Casey Stengel once. I asked him one question and he went on for 28½ minutes.*
>
> Larry King, *Sports Illustrated*

▲ *Paraphrase content.* In your own words, repeat back to the talker what you are hearing, thus encouraging the speaker while making sure that you understand correctly what is being said. Use comments like: "What I am hearing is . . ." or "Are you saying that . . . ?" or "So your feeling is that the Eastern Division will continue to grow?"

▲ *Reflect implications.* Go beyond paraphrasing to see if you are clear about the subtext, ramifications, and implications of what lies behind the speaker's words. Do this with comments like, "Are you suggesting that . . . ?" or "Would that mean . . . ?" or "Does that connect with the need for better service you mentioned earlier?"

▲ *Feed back feelings.* Reflect the underlying feelings you hear being expressed, as a way to get a fuller picture. This is delicate ground, so use tentative comments to express your perceptions. "That must have been rather frustrating . . ." is one comment you might use. Or "Sounds like there was some upset involved . . ." Or "I'll bet it made you really proud that she got promoted."

▲ *Invite further contributions.* If you still have not heard as much as you want, be direct and ask for more. Try comments like, "Could you tell me a little more about . . . ?" or "Please help me understand . . ." or "And what happened then?"

> *Because I love to sell I have to control my impulse to do most of the talking. I work hard at asking good questions and listening with total concentration.*
>
> Chairman, $40-million-a-year marketing company

In active listening, as in all human interaction, the language of the body can be just as important as the language being spoken. Receptive eye contact, a forward-leaning upper-body posture, and well-timed nods of the head all encourage the talker to communicate as fully as possible. An occasional "Um-hum" also helps but most important of all is an attitude of genuinely wanting to learn.

Once you understand listening you are ready to become a student of the fine art of answering questions. One reason this is an art is because many questions, according to social scientists, are not merely requests for information. More than half are actually statements, a significant proportion of which are hostile. Only a minority of the questions you hear, say the experts, are a request for data and nothing else. Sometimes questions are deceptively simple; learning how to decipher and respond to them can be quite complex.

ANSWERING QUESTIONS

Once you understand that, how do you get better at answering questions? Marian Woodall, in her book *Thinking On Your Feet: Answering Questions Well Whether You Know the Answer or Not,* has some useful suggestions:

▲ *Don't just answer, respond.* Answers are often too short or too long, something so brief the questioner is left unsatisfied or so long that it feels like a speech. A response, by contrast, is responsive to the purpose of the questioner and usually consists of the answer plus a support statement—a statistic, an additional piece of information, a quotation, or an opinion.

▲ *Respond to negative questions with positive words.* When a question includes words like *don't, can't, wouldn't,* or *shouldn't,* turn it into a positive statement and then offer an answer in *your* terms. If asked, for example, "Why don't you have more computer experience?" you might answer, "I'm concerned about that too, which is why I'm taking a Pascal course in the evenings. The reason I have less computer experience than I'd like is all the time I've spent training new salespeople."

▲ *When unsure, buy time.* How? The best way is to repeat the question, especially if you focus on the heart of the question. If not overused, silence is also effective, especially if accompanied with a nod or a smile that suggests you are preparing a thoughtful, responsive answer.

▲ *Get a better question.* If a question is particularly difficult, try for a better one. Ask to have the question rephrased, clarified, or defined more sharply. Ask your own question or clarify or define a point yourself.

▲ *"I don't know, but . . ."* There comes a time in each of our lives when we have to admit that we don't know the answer. Rather than bluff and fumble around, try candor. "I don't remember my exact grades in second-year accounting, but I'll check when I get home and phone you with the specifics." Or "I don't recall the sales-increase figure for that year, but I have it in my records and will get it for you this afternoon." We all have times when we don't know the answer, so don't be embarrassed. Just tell the truth and commit to get more precise information, if you possibly can, within a specific time frame.

COACHING TIP

To improve your skill at answering questions, practice with a friend on topics like sports or hobbies. Encourage the friend to ask you what you like and what you do well and why you think that is so. Have you answered your friend's questions completely? How can you be more skillful at answering questions?

One of the most important things to know about answering questions is that you don't have to. Like a presidential candidate or sports celebrity, you can sometimes use a question to offer related information that you feel is more pertinent than what was asked for. Imagine a closing interaction between interviewer and candidate like this:

Interviewer: When could you start?
Candidate: Next Monday. (*Passive answer*)
C: When would you like me to start? (*Better answer*)
C (*Smiling*): Is that a job offer? (*Best answer*)

Instead of providing information, use the question as an opportunity to get a commitment from the interviewer. Transform "When *could* you start?" into a job offer. When asked about your background, frame the answer in terms that relate to the requirements of the job. When asked about your education and training, do the same. When asked about your salary requirements, the response depends on how much you already know.

> *I:* How much money would you expect to earn in this job?
> *C:* Oh, $35 or $40,000. (*Passive answer*)
> *C* (*If you know the range is $40–$45,000*): Something in the neighborhood of $50,000 would seem right to me.
> *C* (*If you don't know the range*): My financial expectations are less important to me right now than the challenges of the job and what I might contribute. Could you give me some idea of the range you have in mind?

Like the "When could you start?" question, questions about money can be signals that a positive decision has been made. That is the time to be professional, responsive, and skillful in getting the kind of offer you want.

Illegal questions require particularly artful responses. You must first know if a question is illegal. (There's a list of such questions at the back of this book that will help you with that.) Then you should consider how your response might affect your chances for being offered the job. For example . . .

> *I:* Are you married?
> *C:* Yes. (*Passive answer*)
> *C* (*If being married is likely to be seen as positive*): Yes, for ten years. And my spouse has been employed by the transit company here for eight years.
> *C* (*If your answer might hurt you*): Is that important in doing the work we are discussing here?

You are not required to answer questions about your age, marital status, sexual preference, nationality, or race. If a question is not job related, you do not have to answer it. If you feel the answer might help your candidacy, by all means offer it and even elaborate. Otherwise, decline politely and move on with the interview.

> *During the lull in between inter-*
> *views, I have the clerk ask*
> *whether the applicant wants in-*
> *dividual, husband-and-wife, or*
> *family coverage, and in choos-*
> *ing an option the candidate will*
> *usually tell the clerk everything*
> *we need to know.*
>
> Anonymous business execu-
> tive quoted in *The Wall Street*
> *Journal*

Be careful about *any* information you give to a prospective employer, whether it is verbal or in writing, to a clerk or a vice president.
A large financial services firm, according to *The Wall Street Journal*,
will take a candidate to lunch at a nice restaurant and casually bring
up the subject of carpooling. The unsuspecting applicant who responds by describing carpooling and sitter problems reduces his or
her chances of getting a job offer.

BUILDING CONFIDENCE

A large component of many questions is the search for reassurance. Hiring people is difficult and mistakes are costly. So interviewers
crave reassurance that you will fit into the organization and solve the
problems you are being hired to solve. They want to have their confidence level raised.

When I was midway through the interviews that led to a ten-year
career as professor of business at a small liberal arts college, the president of the college asked me a number of questions about my recent
employment. I had worked for three companies in the four previous
years, and she was concerned.

"Why did you move so often?" she inquired.

"My training and background are in business," I reminded her.
"But I see now that I am ready for a major change and teaching is
at the heart of it. My jobs in the last four years were the transition
period for arriving here." I reinforced this with a commitment to stay
at the college for at least three years, if offered the job. Apparently
satisfied, it was not long before the president told me that I was the
person they wanted.

Most of us have flat spots in our past, and some of the more
successful people among us have been through awesome failures.

These flat spots and failures can build strong and insightful individuals. Whether an interviewer sees this depends on how the questions are answered.

HOW ABOUT YOU?

What are the questions you might be asked that you could not answer? Think of three before your next interview and spend some time on what you would say if asked those questions. What are the questions you would most hate to be asked? Think of three and, again, spend some time on how you would respond. What are the questions you would most like to be asked? Think of three and then find a way to somehow fit the answers to those questions into your next interview. Then go back to Chapter Sixteen and see if there are important questions you missed.

Coming up with an effective answer to an important question can often turn the tide of an interview in your favor and land you the job you want.

▲

CHAPTER TWENTY-TWO

SUCCESSFUL GROUP
INTERVIEWS

B‌RENT Wilkey needs new employees to help manage the growth of the marketing agency he and his partner run. He wants the best people he can find, he wants to make good use of precious time, and he wants to maximize the involvement of his existing employees in the selection process. So for serious candidates applying for key jobs, Brent Wilkey arranges group interviews.

As a job hunter, you may never face a group interview. But you should be prepared for the possibility, especially if the organization you want to join practices team management or puts special emphasis on collegiality. Group interviews, where you sit with three, four, or five "interviewers," are more formal than interviews in the traditional one-on-one format and usually more stressful. They are often more productive—*if* you know what you are doing.

"Usually there are five of us in the room," says Brent Wilkey, in describing group interviews at his agency, "and it's hard to be anything other than superficial. We worry about overwhelming the candidate, though I don't know why, because we often overwhelm the people already on the job. On balance, group interviews work great for us, because we get so many perspectives in less time than if we did individual interviews. We run the agency as a team, so team interviews make sense."

Currently, the agency is looking for an account supervisor, reports Wilkey, and there are three finalists:

▲ *Raw Talent,* who has great potential for developing into a top performer. This candidate came from Europe, where she sold trinkets on the street to earn money for plane tickets to the United States for herself and her mother. She is the youngest and would also be "the cheapest."

▲ *Client Whiz,* who worked for a company the agency has been serving for two years. This candidate would be more expensive than Raw Talent, and although she has valuable experience, she might have trouble adapting to the agency side of the marketing business.

▲ *Star Competitor,* who worked for a company much like Wilkey's and is a highly skilled presenter, well trained in client management techniques. Wilkey is concerned that she may have been mistrained, however, and could have trouble adjusting to the way things are done in his firm.

Which candidate will be offered the job? Until all are interviewed, Wilkey cannot say. But when asked what he would do if he were interviewed by several people at once, he replied, "I would ask a lot of questions; that's usually a sure bet." Then he added, "And I would listen carefully to the questions asked. I would listen for the thought behind the question and not give simple answers; if they asked me about a place I had worked that had a reputation for weak account management, I would stress the creative work I did there."

> *Some people are motor mouths, they never shut up. I'd like to be able to ask more than one question in an interview.*
>
> Sandra Moersdorf, Recruiting Manager, Procter & Gamble

THE BASICS

The skillful interviewer starts by building rapport and getting agreement on the agenda and timing—a particularly important step when there are several people in the room with different purposes and different roles to play. The skillful interviewer keeps the focus on people issues early in the interview, and then on organizational issues: How would the candidate fit here and how can he or she contribute to meeting the challenges this firm faces? At the end of the interview, the skillful participant—as interviewer or interviewee—looks for closure and is sure that everyone understands what is to happen next.

The group setting is perfect for a participatory interview. As the candidate being interviewed by two or more people in an organization you might join, think: What are the needs and concerns that brought us together today? How can I help to clarify the challenges facing this organization? How can my talents and knowledge and passion be employed to meet these challenges? How can we arrive at the right decision together?

> *If you can talk with crowds and keep your virtue, or walk with kings—nor lose the common touch...*
> Rudyard Kipling, "If"

When you talk with a crowd, remember to keep your virtue—and also your poise and your equanimity. You are there because several people care enough about who they work with to spend this time with you. Let that knowledge inspire you to be as authentic as you can possibly be.

THE DIFFERENCES

The differences between a group and a one-on-one interview are significant. Wilkey points to one of the most important when he says, "I am concerned about the effect of the boss being in the room with four subordinates and a candidate. Can the others really be themselves?" Wilkey, as a managing partner in the firm, has more clout than the rest. When the king is around, things change.

For the candidate, this is crucial information. Who is the senior person in the room? What is his or her relationship to the others? Where does the power lie, and how is it used in this organization? Who will decide on a job offer? Who needs to concur in the decision?

> *During the interview ask questions 20 percent of the time and you will be able to listen 80 percent of the time.*
> Martin John Yate, Advising Employers

You will not be talking 80 percent of the time in most one-on-one job interviews but it can happen when you are facing a group. Be prepared for this. Think beforehand what you want to communicate and what you want to know and who you want to ask questions of.

Jacabo Varela, a Uruguayan psychologist, suggests an effective approach to responding to group decision-making situations. Notice who responds positively, regardless of their relative power in the group, and get that person nodding yes. Then include a second or third ally, and when those people are all coming your way, focus your attention on the senior decision maker. Because of the other supportive reactions in the room, that person is now more likely to respond positively to your candidacy.

There is no doubt that group interviews are more demanding and more complex than one-on-one interviews, and almost always longer.

Is this always negative? Not for everyone. A client of mine says the best interview she ever had was with a group of academics. While the experience was stressful, without question, it was also exhilarating. "It was for a job teaching history at a private academy," she recalls, "and four people were asking me about the French Revolution, all at the same time. It was scary, but great! I loved it!"

> When we interview as a group the candidates like it. They appreciate seeing how we interact, the questions we ask, the byplay.
>
> Margot Fraser, CEO
> Birkenstock Footprint Sandals

On the path to the right work, most of us at one time or another will be interviewed by a team of prospective coworkers. It's helpful to know how to handle this event, which is likely to be similar to the traditional format in some ways and different in others. Be sure that your own planning and participation are good. Remember that in every group interview the basic one-on-one rules apply, only more so, and with some crucial exceptions and additions.

Do everything you can to make sure the important questions get answered, but don't be a motor mouth. Be clear, succinct, and willing to ask, "Did I answer your question?"

Who did Brent Wilkey hire? Was it Raw Talent, Client Whiz, or Star Competitor? As it turns out, the firm hired Star Competitor, and, according to Wilkey, "This person has been just wonderful." Raw Talent is next on the list to hire, and if Client Whiz hadn't dropped out of the running—in part because of an aversion to group interviews—Wilkey thinks they would have eventually hired all three.

CHAPTER TWENTY-THREE

HOW TO SALVAGE A SINKING INTERVIEW

IN the series of interviews that led to my job as a professor and chairman of the Department of Business Administration at a small college, I had several meetings with the dean of the college. He was cordial enough, and curious about what I had learned in talking to similar institutions, but it turned out that he had a particular concern. Or at least it sounded that way.

> *You may have a fresh start any moment you choose, for this thing that we call "failure" is not the falling down, but the staying down.*
> Mary Pickford

"An important part of this job is to build up the business collection in the college library," he told me, "to recommend to the librarian which books to buy and which journals to subscribe to. Have you ever done that?"

The answer was no. I was just completing a fourteen-year career in marketing management, and the only stacks I knew about were piles of product inquiries. But I didn't say no, because I had a sense that this was not a major issue and because I felt it could be handled. What I did say was, "I am familiar with business literature because of my reading and I am familiar with how libraries work, since I have used them all through school as well as professionally." Then the capper: "I am also learning about how libraries work, how collections are created and developed and organized as I earn my Ph.D. . . . and I am sure I could handle this part of the job."

That convinced the dean. It turned out that the college did not have enough money to buy many business volumes anyway. And over ten years, the library was a tiny part of my job. But the dean wanted to feel that he was about to make the right decision. What sounded like a concern was really a request to have his confidence level raised. My response, apparently, gave him that reassurance.

COACHING TIP

Look for ways to demonstrate your reliability. One way is to promise something—to phone or stop by at a specific time—and then do exactly what you promised.

People express their need for reassurance in four ways:

▲ *Questions.* Many questions are really requests for information to erase doubts, to fill the void between the known and the unknown—the person and organizational gaps that create jobs. Respond in terms of satisfying the interviewer's need for greater certainty in his or her decision to choose you for the job you seek.

> Never give up then, for that is just the place and time that the tide will turn.
> Harriet Beecher Stowe

▲ *Concerns.* A little more specific than questions, concerns are negatives that can be given a name. "I'm wondering about your lack of experience in computers" is a concern and so is "I'm a little worried about the sales results in your last assignment." This request for reassurance should be met with specific information—statistics, examples, opinions, followed by an expression of what you believe you can do.

▲ *Objections.* Several degrees more serious than concerns, objections are major issues. If not responded to, objections can deny you the job offer. The classic reasons given are, "You do not have enough experience" and "You are overqualified." Others include, "You do not have a college degree" and "I don't think you would fit in here" (because of age, gender, or other unstated differences). For this kind of objection, the right response is to focus on how well you can do the job, based on your understanding of your own experience and interests. Objections are not insurmountable, if handled promptly.

> *You ain't going nowhere, son, expect back to driving trucks.*
> Manager of Grand Ole Opry to Elvis Presley after his first performance

▲ *Rejections.* "No" or "No way!" or even, "Sorry" are hard for us to hear, even harder to accept. Sometimes such rejections are an authentic expression of a considered opinion, but often they are a request for reassurance, and we don't know for sure until we check it out. A man I know flew to Boston the day after getting his rejection letter from the Harvard Business School and called from Logan Airport to ask to see the Director of Admissions. "I think you've made a mistake, sir," he told the bemused official, and an hour later the decision had been reversed. Never a great student, this tenacious young man nevertheless finished the two-year course and went on to a successful business career. Like him, we do not have to accept rejection the first time, or even the second, and sometimes not ever.

Whatever kind of roadblock we are responding to, whether it's a concern or even a rejection, there are two essential steps to responding.

> *Very early in my work as a therapist, I discovered that simply listening to my client, very attentively, was an important way of being useful.*
> Carl Rogers

RESPONDING WELL

The first step is to listen. We need to hear accurately and fully what is being said to us. We must actively engage in the listening process by paraphrasing content, reflecting implications, feeding back feelings, inviting further contributions, or whatever else is appropriate to that situation.

The second step is to take the initiative. Rather than passively accepting what is put in our path and bringing our lives to a halt, we must move ahead.

In responding, we must think like the person with whom we are talking. What information is being sought? What is the real concern here? What fears lurk behind objections? Ask yourself: "If I were in his shoes, what would be going on in my head?" We need to think and respond as though we were a partner in the process, concerned that the end result is right for both parties. Like Carl Rogers, we need to look for ways to be useful.

COACHING TIP

One way to buy time for handling objections is to be candid about your reaction. "Ouch, that hurts!" And then, "Could you help me understand your concern?"

The best way to respond is before a concern is even expressed. If your research indicates that a college degree is highly valued in the organization you want to join, acknowledge that openly. "I know that most people you hire have a B.A.," you might say. "And I want you to know that I was traveling and working in Europe while most of my contemporaries were getting their degrees. That gave me a cultural sensitivity that might be important in a multinational company like this. Plus, with my work history and the professional courses I have taken, I bring you both the talent and the motivation to do this job."

TRANSFORMING OBJECTIONS

One of the best ways to respond once a concern has been expressed is with the feel, felt, found sequence. "I understand how you feel about my educational background. My first employer felt the same way. What he found was that my skills and dedication to the job were more important than the number of college units I had." The first sentence acknowledges feelings, the second reinforces the first with an example, and the third gives a specific response. Try it, the next time you encounter an objection. You will discover that the feel, felt, found sequence is a powerful way to respond in an interview.

This approach works with other senses too. For the visually dominant, it is "I see what you mean; others saw it that way too; now they look at it differently." For those for whom sound is most important, "I know what you are hearing; others heard it that way too; now they are singing a different tune." Where mental processes dominate, it is "I understand what you are thinking; others thought that way too; now they think about it differently." Use your own words and the language appropriate to the situation, of course, but remember this three-step sequence for handling concerns.

> *Success is going from failure to*
> *failure with great enthusiasm.*
> Winston Churchill

SAVING THE INTERVIEW

What do you do when it seems that all is lost? That despite all your preparation and practice, you are in serious trouble? It all depends:

▲ If the interviewer becomes silent and is not participating, ask questions to find out what is happening. Is there more that the person would like to know? Other topics to cover? Anything else they could tell you about the company? Is the interviewer ready to conclude? Probe for the problem and look for ways to reengage the person across the desk.

▲ If the interviewer won't stop talking, find a space and gently interrupt. "Excuse me," you might say, "but I want to be sure you get a chance to hear about some of my accomplishments that relate to this job." Use questions to get the focus right. Remind the interviewer of the agenda. Take action. Initiate.

▲ If you get asked the question you most hate to hear, restate it more positively (using strategies from the last chapter) and give an answer that links to the needs of the company. Thorough preparation makes the difference!

▲ If the interview is interrupted, make the best of it. Profit from the interruption by collecting your thoughts, observing things you may have missed before, and listening to what is being said. If the interviewer's boss has walked into the room (as happened once to me), take the opportunity to introduce yourself.

▲ If you have said all you have to say and asked all your questions and there are still twenty minutes to go, say goodbye. But first get agreement on what is to happen next—a written job offer or more interviews or a phone callback from you—and then express your appreciation for the time spent. People appreciate people who respect the value of time.

▲ If the interviewer turns rude partway through, probe for the problem. Was it something you said? Does a point need to be clarified? Has it been a bad day? An honest emotional response, sympathy or even anger, is often best in a situation like this.

▲ If you discover that the person you are talking to is not really the right person, make the best of it. Learn what you can, ask for help in connecting with a more appropriate person, and move on. There are no accidents in life, so get full use out of any situation you find yourself in.

W. C. Fields once said, "If at first you don't succeed, try, try again. Then quit. There's no use being a damn fool about it." When it seems that all is lost, it's time to move on to other challenges, pursue other jobs at other companies or other careers in other fields. The most successful people are ready when this time comes because they have developed work and career options for themselves.

> *It doesn't matter if you don't always hit the exact bull's-eye. The other rings in the target score points too.*
>
> A. P. Giannini, Founder, Bank of America

Recognize that even though the outcome was not what you had in mind, you can learn from the experience and hone skills that will help you next time. Like A. P. Giannini, you may not hit the bull's-eye every time, but you will score points if you try often enough. After each interview, make a note in your "Lessons Learned" journal and take pride in the progress you are making.

But don't give up and move on too soon. Don't quit before you have responded as effectively as you possibly can to the concerns and objections you encounter in your search for the right work. Give yourself every possible chance to be successful. Remember that however painful your feelings of rejection may be, they are less important than your dedication to making the most of your talent and passion.

▲

CHAPTER TWENTY-FOUR

THE CAPPER

CLARE Boothe Luce wrote her first book, *Stuffed Shirts*, a collection of satirical stories about New York society, when she was twenty-seven. Determined to pursue a writing career, she approached a social friend, Condé Nast, owner of *Vogue* and *Vanity Fair*. "I know your type, Clare," he told her when she asked for a job. "The first time you get a glamorous invitation to Palm Beach, you'll be off."

Nast then sailed for Europe and, according to Ms. Luce, forgot the whole thing; she, however, went to *Vogue*, sat down at an empty desk, and acted as if she had been hired. When the week's paychecks were distributed and there was no envelope for her, Ms. Luce chalked it up to Nast's forgetfulness.

By the time Nast returned, six weeks later, Ms. Luce had so impressed Donald Freeman, *Vanity Fair*'s managing editor, that he made her an assistant editor. Within three years, she established herself as a major force at the magazine and was elevated to managing editor.

What can we learn from Clare Boothe Luce? That success comes to those who express their determination to get the job by words and by actions. Her only interview for this job was her conversation with her friend Condé Nast, and the main event was asking for a job. She got the job she asked for because of her boldness, her persistence, and her belief in herself.

Whatever precedes that magic moment when the job is yours, whether it is months of interviews or a single conversation, nothing happens until the close. Most of us are not audacious enough to sit down at the desk without an offer, but all of us can demonstrate that we want to be hired, as the heroine in this story did. Her actions may not be your actions, but her attitude is worth emulating.

There are many ways to get jobs and many kinds of job interviews. All involve taking action, as Clare Boothe Luce did; not one is successful without initiative. Some job opportunities may come as unsolicited offers, but unless you display a positive response, nothing will happen.

If an interview is like a pyramid, the climactic moment is when the capstone is added.

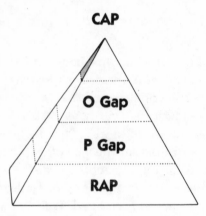

The word *cap* is also a way to remember three issues that must be addressed at the end of an interview. Closure, Appreciation, and Procedures—CAP. Of the three, the first is the most important.

> *What I hear more and more often these days from my senior managers is, "How do we get candidates to say yes to our job offers?"*
> President, $35-million-a-year retailer

CLOSING

Closure is the joint process of finding the right conclusion to the interview. We all want closure in our human interactions. We all want a sense of completion, even if it is just a cordially expressed farewell. At the end of a job-seeking interview, if you are sure that this is the job you want, the right closure for you is a job offer. If you are on the other side of the desk, and at the end of an interview you think you have found the right person to fill a position, closure for you is acceptance of your job offer then and there . . . or certain acceptance within a very short time after the interview.

> Look for shared interests and
> differing interests to dovetail.
> Seek to make their decision
> easy.
>
> Roger Fisher and William Ury,
> Getting to Yes

If both sides have participated fully in the interview it should be apparent at closure where your interests differ and where they dovetail.

Be prepared to take the initiative at closure time. This is scary, because the risk of rejection is high, but it is essential. For good things to happen, people must ask for what they want.

There are many ways to achieve closure, but the five most important in a job interview are these:

▲ *Summing up.* The most natural way to conclude is with a question like, "How does all this sound to you?" That can be preceded by a review of all that has gone before, both about the job and about your qualifications for it. Other concluding questions are, "Does this make sense to you?" or "What do you think?"

▲ *T account.* One way to sum up is to create a T account like the ones you may have done in figuring out what work is right for you. Take a sheet of paper and draw a line across the top. Above it write, "Should you hire me?" Now draw a line perpendicular to the first, down the center of the page, forming a large T. On the left at the top write "Yes" and below list all the reasons you are the right person for the job. On the right, under "No," put possible problems. The longer list on the left suggests the right way to conclude the interview, and at that point you ask for agreement. The T account can also be a mental picture, so even if you do not use a piece of paper, be adding to the "Yes" list in the mind of the interviewer. Like the T account exercise described in Chapter Four, this clarifies the decision-making process.

> ## COACHING TIP
>
> Practice closing with a friend on some small matter, like which movie to go to or what to have for dinner. Tell them this is practice and ask for their advice on how you might do it better. Repeat this process tomorrow. Repeat ten times: "I will get better at asking for what I want."

▲ *Yes, yes, yes.* Part of why the T account is successful is that it gets people thinking yes, yes, yes. The way this works is to ask something like, "Do you agree that my college training is right for this job?" and then, "And my experience fits what you are looking for?" and finally, "Doesn't it seem that I am the right person for this job?" When people say yes once and then twice they are far more likely to say it a third and fourth time, especially when you are helping them overcome inertia and get what they really want.

▲ *Minor point.* Making a job offer is a major decision, so an applicant can sometimes make it easier for the interviewer by focusing on just one piece of that decision. This involves questions like, "From your standpoint, when would be the best time for me to start?" or "Could you give me an idea of where my office would be?" Often the minor point is the not-so-minor question of compensation. You may be asked about a salary range, and the way to close at that point is to follow your dollar response with "How does that work for you?"

▲ *Short supply.* Good people are always in short supply and good organizations know it. If you have job offers, or even the possibility of offers, from other employers it is sometimes useful to make that known. This is a time for honesty, however, not arrogance. So indicate that you must let another company know by the tenth, if that is so, but do it in a matter-of-fact way.

Because closure is a scary prospect for even the most experienced interviewees, there is a tendency to keep on talking as a way to avoid or postpone hearing the answer. Resist the tendency. Ask the key question in whatever form is right for you and stay silent until you hear the answer.

Your skill at closing the interview will not only help you get the work you want, it will also demonstrate to those with whom you talk that you are a professional, skilled in the interpersonal processes that all organizations respect.

Well-managed organizations respect candor, especially at closing time; if you want the job, say so. If you are agonizing over two choices, let them know. If you are probably going to accept another offer, don't mislead a prospective employer by implying that you are going to sign on.

APPRECIATION

No interview, however frustrating, should conclude without an expression of thanks—for the time spent, the information offered, the opportunities presented. Express your gratitude for the positive aspects of the interview. Applaud the contributions of the person across the desk from you. Congratulate both of you on what has been accomplished.

Appreciation expressed face-to-face is good, but it is even better when reinforced with a thank-you note. You read in Chapter Thirteen about the value of sending such letters, especially when they go out the day of the interview. It is a personalized communication that puts your name before an important decision maker—for the second or third time. The thank-you note also gives you a chance to reiterate key points from the interview, as in the example below:

Your home address
City, state, & zip
Your phone number
Today's date

Ms./Mr. Full name, title
Correct company name
Correct address

Dear Ms./Mr. _____:

It was good meeting with you today to discuss the sales associate position you are filling. Thank you for being so forthcoming in our interview.

On reflection, I am more convinced than ever that my computer store sales experience and my marketing courses at State qualify me to be successful in this job. I am highly motivated and feel certain I can exceed your performance expectations if you choose to give me the opportunity.

I will phone later this week to find out if you have further questions and to see if there is anything else I can do to convince you to say yes.

Sincerely,

Your full name

A San Francisco police officer in one of my workshops called me six months later and said, "You remember that job in the DA's office I was going for? Well, I got it.

"And you know what made the difference? It was the thank-you note I sent. You told us to *always* send a thank-you note, so I did. The district attorney who hired me said it was the first one he ever received from a job applicant."

Jay Levinson is sure that he got his job at the Leo Burnett advertising agency because he sent thank-you notes to every one of the seven people he met on the interview trail there. "I tried to include something personal in each note," he recalls, "and I know that made a difference."

> **The thankful receiver bears a plentiful harvest.**
> **William Blake**

WHAT HAPPENS NEXT?

Procedures come last in capping the interview. You need to agree on what happens next. Are they going to send you a letter confirming their offer? Make sure you know when it will be mailed. Are you going to let them know your decision? Make sure you agree on the date. Are you to meet some other people in the organization? Make sure you know who, their positions in the firm, when the meeting is to take place, and who is responsible for the arrangements.

Procedures is the action part of closure. Without agreement on procedures, the interview is incomplete.

One important procedure to do on your own is to make notes when you leave the interview, for your file on this prospective employer or for your "Lessons Learned" journal.

FOLLOW-UP

If you leave the interview without a job offer, your work is not finished. Closure is not complete until you have the work options you seek.

Your willingness to follow up benefits you, yes, but also your prospective employer. The number-one candidate, the one who just edged you out, may have turned down the offer. Or a new, perhaps better, job may have opened up in the short time since you walked out the door. Organizations are crying out for people who persevere. Be one of those people.

Contrary to popular belief, there is a lot you can do to improve your chances for getting the job for which you just interviewed. Rather than sit at home and worry, try one or more of these three follow-up strategies, requiring only a phone call and a back-up letter or visit:

▲ *More thorough answer.* If there was a question in the interview that you did not answer to your satisfaction, call back and fill in the blanks. You might say something like, "When you asked about my accounting experience, I mentioned my classes at State but not the evening course I took last winter. Also, as treasurer of my club, I am actively involved in accounting applications." Take this opportunity to add, "I feel strongly that I could contribute to your company's growth. Is there anything more I can do to demonstrate this?"

> *Active recruiters collect good résumés and they collect good people. Your second choice for a particular job could very well be your first choice for a job opening you didn't know you'd have.*
>
> Robin Bradford, Personnel Agency Owner

▲ *Additional solutions.* If you have a new idea on how you might contribute, call back and say something like, "After we talked about your new sales incentive program, I began thinking that some of what I learned in the gain-sharing plan at Apex might apply to your situation." Then, "May I put these ideas in writing and drop them off, say tomorrow at 4:30?" Use the follow-up visit to again express your interest in the position and ask for a chance to put your talent to work.

▲ *New information.* If your reading or networking turns up something that might be of interest to your prospective employer, use that as a reason to call back. "I noticed your interest in Just-In-Time inventory management," you might say, "and wonder if you have seen the article in next month's *Forbes.*" Then, "May I drop a copy off this afternoon?" Use your own words, but make sure you connect and make sure you are clear about your interest in the job.

The reason you follow up is to give both you *and* the organization another chance. You both get additional feedback, both get another opportunity to review the decision.

There's one more reason for a return visit, according to Ann Landers, who gave this advice to "I Live in Boston":

> *People who strike out on job interviews should go back to some of the places where they failed and ask the person with whom they spoke why they weren't hired and how to make a better presentation. If they listen carefully, they are sure to improve their chances.*

Follow-up is essential because your job search is not complete until you have found the work you want. The pyramid is not complete until the peak is in place.

COACHING TIP

If your job search bogs down, go back and review the nine steps to knowing your right work. This will allow you to integrate new insights, clarify your direction, and renew your inspiration.

Never give up.
Never, Never, Never give up.
Winston Churchill

10

NEVER GIVE UP

A bright, eager student in one of my classes tells a story that speaks volumes about how to cap an interview. Several years ago, he was living in Phoenix where, following a tour in Viet Nam, he got a job as an investigator for the Arizona Commission for Alcoholic Beverage Control. But he wanted more. He wanted to be in business, even though his father was a schoolteacher and no one in his family had ever been in business. And he wanted to be in sales, even though he had never sold before. And he wanted to be in sales for IBM.

When he went to the IBM district office and filled out an application, the receptionist said, "I believe you missed something here, the part where it says college degree."

"I have no college degree," he said.

She rolled her eyes. "We'll call you."

Undaunted, he went out and talked to IBM salespeople and IBM customers. He read everything he could find on IBM, written by the company and others, favorable to the company and hostile. He visited the office sixteen times over the next fourteen months and talked with everyone, always asking for the kind of interview that could lead to his being offered a job.

When his perseverance paid off, he was ready. When he got to the crucial point in the interview with the manager who could hire him, the moment when the job offer would either happen or not happen, he took the initiative.

"Look," he said, "if you're going to hire me because I'm black, I'll sit here all day long and be as black as anyone you could hire. No one could possibly be blacker than me.

"But if you're going to hire me because I can sell the products and services of this division, then there is only one thing you could do better than hiring me." He smiled.

"And that is to hire two just like me."

Bill Smith got the job and has been in the IBM 100% Sales Club every year since. He showed that any of us can overcome handicaps—education, race, or whatever our own particular variety may be—if we will prepare, persevere, and cap off the interview with confidence and candor.

▲

CHAPTER TWENTY-FIVE

WHEN CAN YOU START?

W HEN Bill Smith was pursuing a job with IBM he was clear about his goal. He knew he wanted to be in business, he knew he wanted to be in sales, and he knew what company he wanted to work for. He met with success because he prepared well, because he persevered against all obstacles, and because he kept his target clearly in sight.

We too can succeed in our search for the right work if we keep our targets clearly in sight, and if we remember the seven cardinal rules of interviewing.

1.   *Be honest, always.* Those who succeed at work, long term, are honest. Those who participate fully as team members are honest. Those who are honest meet with success and can view their accomplishments with pride.

What is honesty? First and foremost, it is being truthful with ourselves. It is being perceptive about our changing talent, knowledge, and passion. It is being aware of our limitations and balancing that awareness with a healthy skepticism for the voice that whispers to us in the night, "You can't do it . . . you're a phony." Don't heed that voice. Listen, listen, listen for the truth about yourself. Dig deep inside for what is positive and authentic.

From inner honesty comes honesty with others. Always tell the truth. Avoid exaggeration. Tell it like it is, and support it with real facts, true examples, and authentic opinions. You do not need to reveal your every wart and blemish, but never tell an untruth.

Honesty is not easy. When we desperately want an interview or a job, the temptation to mislead or exaggerate is great. It is essential, however, to resist. Any short-term gain will be lost in later erosion of trust and in eventual disillusionment.

2. *Initiate, participate, engage fully.* We are judged by how we participate in an interview. When we initiate and display a willingness to lead, we are providing a preview of how we would perform on the job in the months and years ahead. If we initiate, we get the best interview results for ourselves and those on the other side of the desk. If we initiate, we are more likely to bring the best of our talent, knowledge, and passion into play in the world.

> *Keep your network active and expanding. Individuals who are regularly in touch with large numbers of people, even if they do not know them well, have the best access to job openings.*
>
> Barbara Block, Career Consulting

Stay connected to the people in your world, particularly your work world. Initiate with them, participate with them, seek them out during your job search and afterward. There is no better resource than friends, and none more dependable.

3. *If in doubt, check it out.* Remember George Keller's advice from Chapter Twenty-one and never underestimate the value of an intelligent question. Show the courage to ask for more information. Make the effort to achieve clarity. Avoid obscurity and obfuscation. If you are not sure where you stand, the other person may have the same problem. Check it out.

4. *Think like an owner.* Be involved, always. Think like an owner of resources, especially human resources, especially your own. Think like an owner of problems: *our* problems, not your problems or my problems. And finally, think like the owner or owners of the organization. If it were your money invested, would you want someone like you to work for the organization? Be sure the answer is yes!

5. *Flex, bend, rebound.* Be like John Sculley when he was talking to Apple Computers in New York and in California, in Central Park and in a record store. At first Sculley didn't even want to work for Apple, but he was open, responsive, curious, and flexible. And eventually successful.

Like all human interactions, and more than most, interviewing requires flexibility. Read the other person and adjust your communication style accordingly. Hear the needs of the other person and respond to those needs. Rebound from the rejections that will surely come with all the talent, knowledge, and passion you can muster.

As you flex, bend, and rebound, maintain your integrity. You are bigger than any single interchange, any single interview, any single rejection. Remember who you are. Remember your purpose.

> You can fly, but that cocoon has got to go.
>
> Michael Larsen (Seen on a poster)

6. *When in trouble, return to purpose.* When your plans go awry and the person across from you doesn't seem to listen or even care, remember why you are there. Take a moment to think about why you are in that particular interview, what work you are seeking, and what you want to do with your life. Then rejoin the process with a fresh perspective and renewed energy. Persevere. You *will* succeed.

Like Bill Smith, put your mission ahead of your skin color or education or other real and imagined handicaps. Put your gifts ahead of your hurt feelings or embarrassment or depression. Remember your purpose.

7. *Continue learning, every day.* "Learn as though you were going to live forever," as Johnny Wooden says. Wherever you are in life you will be using at least some of your interviewing skills again, probably to get another job. The skills and knowledge you develop in becoming a proficient interviewer are some of the most important assets you will ever have.

> Be amazing. The more amazing you are, the more you will succeed.
>
> Jay Levinson

Remember that you will use these assets not just in finding work but in doing work. You will use them as you sit on the other side of the interviewing desk, as you participate in meetings at work, and as you negotiate the agreements that make you a valued employee. These assets are not a one-time thing, like a candle that burns and goes out. They endure for a lifetime. They offer ongoing light.

Remember that no one person, not even the wisest, knows all there is to know about human interactions. But all of us can learn as we go down the path.

Jay Levinson, the star on the interviewing trail at Leo Burnett advertising, remembers the founder. "I was leaving for a new assignment in Europe and when I said goodbye to Leo he gave me a big hug and said, 'I wish I were you.' When I asked him why, this advertising giant, a man who had scaled the peak of his profession, said, 'So I could start all over again.' "

Leo Burnett is no longer alive, but the motto that shaped his life and his advertising agency endures for us all: "If you reach for the stars, you may not get one, but you won't come up with a handful of mud, either."

In interviewing, reach for the stars. Reach for the best that is in you and in those around you. Be prepared, be ready to participate fully in whatever happens, be willing to be successful. Aim for the ultimate interview. Tune your ear for those magic words, "When can you start?"

▲

Appendix

What a Skillful Interviewer Does
Before, During, and After

ONE. *Before the interview:*

▲ Prepares a position description, stating the mission of the job, main responsibilities, and reporting relationships.

▲ Prepares a job specification, describing the experience, motivations, values, and beliefs of the ideal candidate.

▲ Prepares an organizational chart, showing where the new person fits, now and three years from now.

▲ Reviews the candidate's file: résumé, references, and reports (verbal and written) of others who have talked to him or her.

TWO. *During the interview:*

▲ Establishes rapport right from the outset. Puts the candidate at ease.

▲ Assesses the personal "chemistry." How would this person fit?

▲ Assesses the match between the challenges in this job and the skills, knowledge, and passion of the candidate.

▲ Ends the interview with closure on the main issues and a clear understanding of next steps.

THREE. *After the interview:*

▲ Records impressions and agreements in interview notes.

▲ Completes the reference check, if appropriate.

▲ Sends a follow-up letter, whether there is an offer or not.

▲ Follows up. If this is the right candidate, pursues until the answer is yes!

INTERVIEW GUIDE—THEIR QUESTIONS

What they want to know:	Will you fit in?	Are you motivated?	Will you produce?	Will you work out?
Questions they will ask:	Tell me about yourself.	How much do you know about our business or service?	What could you do for us?	Why did you leave your last position?
	What are your strengths?	What skills would you like to put to use here?	What are your strengths?	Are you settled in this community?
	What are your weaknesses?	Where would you like to be five (or ten) years from now?	What are your weaknesses?	Are you willing to relocate?
	What have you learned from your successes? From your setbacks?	What does excellence mean to you?	What are your most important achievements?	What are your compensation expectations? Now? Three years from now?
	If your last boss was telling a friend all about you, what would he or she say?		What is the best thing about you?	
			What is the worst?	

What to tell them:	What you are like (being guided by how revealing and expressive they are) How you have fit in elsewhere How you believe you would fit in here	What motivates you in the work being discussed What has motivated you in the past How your passion in other parts of your life links to this work	Examples of achievements that relate to this organization Relevant strengths and relevant nonweaknesses Illustrations of tenacity, commitment, & endurance Statement of your belief about your ability to produce	Examples of how you worked out in previous jobs What you are willing to commit to this job, in time and energy How long you would commit to staying in the job Compensation expectations—only if they are unwilling to name figures first
Where to look for help:	"Wishes," pp. 4–7 "Values," pp. 14–16 "Tell me about yourself" pp. 90–94 Ch. 21	"Likes," pp. 9–11 "Priorities," pp. 22–24 "Collecting Information," pp. 54–56 Ch. 21	"Experience," pp. 7–8 "Collecting Information," pp. 54–56 Ch. 21	"Money," pp. 20–22 How much would you expect to earn? pp. 126–27 "Gifts," pp. 11–13 "Priorities," pp. 22–24 Ch. 21

INTERVIEW GUIDE—YOUR QUESTIONS

What you want to know:	Will I fit in?	Are the challenges right?	Are the conditions right?	Are the rewards right?
What to ask:	What do you look for in people who join this organization? What kinds of people do best here? How are new people acclimated here?	What are the main responsibilities of this job? Why is this job open? What really needs to be done here? If you got the ideal person in this job, what would you expect to be his or her most significant achievement?	What kinds of resources are available to do this job? What is the work environment like? What are the workday expectations? How important is teamwork?	How do you reward your successful people? What nonfinancial rewards can people expect here? If I asked ten people, "What's the best thing about working here?" what would they say? What kind of programs do you have to help me get better at my job?

	Job specification	Position description		
What to look for:	Common values, common beliefs, common attitudes Revealing stories Other clues to the culture	Clues to what makes the organization succeed, e.g., where do profits come from? Hidden challenges—difficult bosses, money problems, organizational discontent	Where is the work done? By what kinds of people? Using what work styles? For what purposes? Is it too big? Too small? How about work-group size? What can be learned from company literature? From articles on the company or its competitors?	Flexibility on reward systems Willingness to negotiate on compensation Unorthodox reward systems Plaques on walls, trophies, letters of commendation Training programs, support for outside study, opportunities to learn new skills
Where to look for help:	"Wishes," pp. 4–7 Ch. 9 Ch. 16	Ch. 19 Ch. 20	"Wishes," pp. 4–7 "Priorities," pp. 22–24 Ch. 9	"Money," pp. 20–22 How much would you expect to earn? pp. 126–27 "Likes," pp. 9–11

PREEMPLOYMENT INQUIRY GUIDELINES

SUBJECT	ACCEPTABLE	UNACCEPTABLE
NAME	Name "Have you ever used another name? *or* "Is any additional information relative to change of name, use of an assumed name, or nickname necessary to enable a check on your work and education record? If yes, please explain."	Maiden name
RESIDENCE	Place of residence.	"Do you own or rent your home?"
AGE	Statement that hire is subject to verification that applicant meets legal age requirements. "If hired can you show proof of age?" "Are you over eighteen years of age?" "If under eighteen, can you, after employment, submit a work permit?"	Age. Birthdate. Dates of attendance or completion of elementary or high school. Questions which tend to identify applicants over age 40.
BIRTHPLACE, CITIZENSHIP	"Can you, after employment, submit verification of your legal right to work in the United States?" *or* Statement that such proof may be required after employment.	Birthplace of applicant, applicant's parents, spouse, or other relatives. "Are you a U.S. citizen?" *or* Citizenship of applicant, applicant's parents, spouse, or other relatives. Requirements that applicant produce naturalization, first papers, or alien card *prior to employment.*

NATIONAL ORIGIN	Languages applicant reads, speaks, or writes, if use of a language other than English is relevant to the job for which applicant is applying.	Questions as to nationality, lineage, ancestry, national origin, descent, or parentage of applicant, applicant's parents, or spouse. "What is your mother tongue?" or Language commonly used by applicant. How applicant acquired ability to read, write, or speak a foreign language.
SEX, MARITAL STATUS, FAMILY	Name and address of parent or guardian if applicant is a minor. Statement of company policy regarding work assignment of employees who are related.	Questions which indicate applicant's sex. Questions which indicate applicant's marital status. Number and/or ages of children or dependents. Provisions for child care. Questions regarding pregnancy, child bearing, or birth control. Name or address of relative, spouse, or children of adult applicant. "With whom do you reside?" or "Do you live with your parents?"
RACE, COLOR		Questions as to applicant's race or color. Questions regarding applicant's complexion or color of skin, eyes, hair.

PREEMPLOYMENT INQUIRY GUIDELINES

SUBJECT	ACCEPTABLE	UNACCEPTABLE
PHYSICAL DESCRIPTION, PHOTOGRAPH	Statement that photograph may be required after employment.	Questions as to applicant's height and weight.
		Require applicant to affix a photograph to application.
		Request applicant, at his or her option, to submit a photograph.
		Require a photograph after interview but before employment.
PHYSICAL CONDITION, HANDICAP	Statement by employer that offer may be made contingent on applicant passing a job-related physical examination.	Questions regarding applicant's general medical condition, state of health, or illnesses.
		Questions regarding receipt of Workers' Compensation.
	"Do you have any physical condition or handicap which may limit your ability to perform the job applied for? If yes, what can be done to accommodate your limitation?"	"Do you have any physical disabilities or handicaps?"
RELIGION	Statement by employer of regular days, hours, or shifts to be worked.	Questions regarding applicant's religion.
		Religious days observed or "Does your religion prevent you from working weekends or holidays?"
ARREST, CRIMINAL RECORD	"Have you ever been convicted of a felony?" Such a question must be accompanied by a statement that a conviction will not necessarily disqualify an applicant from employment.	Arrest record or "Have you ever been arrested?"

BONDING	Statement that bonding is a condition of hire.	Questions regarding refusal or cancellation of bonding.
MILITARY SERVICE	Questions regarding relevant skills acquired during applicant's U.S. military service.	General questions regarding military service, such as dates and type of discharge. Questions regarding service in a foreign military.
ECONOMIC STATUS		Questions regarding applicant's current or past assets, liabilities, or credit rating, including bankruptcy or garnishment.
ORGANIZATIONS, ACTIVITIES	"Please list job-related organizations, clubs, professional societies, or other associations to which you belong—you may omit those which indicate your race, religious creed, color, national origin, ancestry, sex, or age."	"List all organizations, clubs, societies, and lodges to which you belong."
REFERENCES	"By whom were you referred for a position here?" Names of persons willing to provide professional and/or character references for applicant.	Questions of applicant's former employers or acquaintances which elicit information specifying the applicant's race, color, religious creed, national origin, ancestry, physical handicap, medical condition, marital status, age, or sex.
NOTICE IN CASE OF EMERGENCY	Name and address of person to be notified in case of accident or emergency.	Name and address of relative to be notified in case of accident or emergency.

These guidelines, developed for Californians by the State of California Department of Fair Employment and Housing, cover most illegal questions under state and federal law in the United States. Because laws change, however, and court interpretations vary, these should not be viewed as an exhaustive compilation of acceptable and unacceptable inquiries for any part of the country.

▲

BIBLIOGRAPHY

Bloch, Barbara, *How to Have a Winning Job Interview*, National Textbook Company, Chicago. 1987.

Bolles, Richard, *The Three Boxes of Life*, Ten Speed Press, Berkeley. 1978.

———, *What Color Is Your Parachute?* Ten Speed Press, Berkeley. 1981.

Bradford, Robin, *The Joy of Job Hunting*, Bradford Personnel Press, San Francisco. 1985.

———, *The Hire IQ*, Bradford Personnel Press, San Francisco. 1989.

Brady, John, *The Craft of Interviewing*, Random House, New York. 1977.

Caple, John, *Careercycles*, Prentice Hall Press, New York. 1983.

———, *The Right Work*, Dodd, Mead & Company, New York. 1987.

DePree, Max, *Leadership Is an Art*, Doubleday, New York. 1989.

Fisher, Roger, and Ury, William, *Getting to Yes*, Houghton Mifflin, Boston. 1981.

Hawken, Paul, *Growing a Business*, Simon & Schuster, New York. 1988.

Hellman, Paul, *Ready, Aim, You're Hired!* Amacom Press, New York. 1986.

Jackson, Tom, *Guerrilla Tactics in the Job Market*, Bantam Books, New York. 1978.

———, *The Perfect Resume*, Doubleday, New York. 1990.

Kennedy, Jim, *Getting Behind the Resume*, Prentice Hall Information Services, Paramus, N.J. 1987.

Krannich, Caryl, and Krannich, Ronald, *Interview for Success*, Impact Publications, Manassas, Va. 1988.

Levinson, Jay, *Quit Your Job!* Dodd, Mead & Company, New York. 1987.

———, *555 Ways to Earn Extra Money*, Henry Holt & Company, New York. 1990.

———, Earning Money Without a Job, Henry Holt & Company, New York. 1991.

Maddux, Robert, *Quality Interviewing*, Crisp Publications, Los Altos, Calif. 1988.

Medley, Anthony, *Sweaty Palms*, Ten Speed Press, Berkeley. 1978.

Merman, S., and McLaughlin, J., *Outinterviewing the Interviewer*, Prentice Hall Press, New York. 1986.

Molloy, John, *Dress for Success,* Warner Books, New York. 1976.

——, *Molloy's New Dress for Success,* Warner Books, New York. 1988.

——, *The Woman's Dress for Success Book,* Warner Books, New York. 1978.

Nierenberg, Gerrald and Calero, Henry, *How to Read a Person Like a Book,* Pocket Books, New York. 1971.

Panté, Robert, *Dressing to Win,* Doubleday, New York. 1984.

Parker, Yana, *The Damn Good Resume Guide,* Ten Speed Press, Berkeley. 1989.

Phillips, Michael, *The Seven Laws of Money,* Random House, New York. 1974.

Sculley, John, with Byrne, John, *Odyssey,* Harper and Row, New York. 1987.

Sher, Barbara, *Wishcraft,* Ballantine Books, New York. 1979.

Siegelman, Ellen, *Personal Risk,* Harper and Row, New York. 1983.

Simon, Sidney, et al., *Values Clarification,* Hart Publishing Company, New York. 1972.

Sinetar, Marsha, *Do What You Love, The Money Will Follow,* Dell Publishing, New York. 1987.

Wallach, Ellen, *The Job Search Companion,* Harvard Common Press, Boston. 1984.

Yate, Martin John, *Hiring the Best,* Bob Adams, Inc., Boston. 1987.

Author's Note

Like those he advises, the author aims to continue learning. If you have comments or suggestions for future editions of *The Ultimate Interview,* please write:

John Caple
523 Fourth Street #206
San Rafael, CA 94901

Your input is important. Thank you.

Index